If the Truth Be Told

Social Fictions Series

Series Editor
Patricia Leavy
USA

The *Social Fictions* series emerges out of the arts-based research movement. The series includes full-length fiction books that are informed by social research but written in a literary/artistic form (novels, plays, and short story collections). Believing there is much to learn through fiction, the series only includes works written entirely in the literary medium adapted. Each book includes an academic introduction that explains the research and teaching that informs the book as well as how the book can be used in college courses. The books are underscored with social science or other scholarly perspectives and intended to be relevant to the lives of college students—to tap into important issues in the unique ways that artistic or literary forms can.

Please email queries to pleavy7@aol.com

International Editorial Advisory Board

Carl Bagley, University of Durham, UK
Anna Banks, University of Idaho, USA
Carolyn Ellis, University of South Florida, USA
Rita Irwin, University of British Columbia, Canada
J. Gary Knowles, University of Toronto, Canada
Laurel Richardson, The Ohio State University (Emeritus), USA

If the Truth Be Told

Accounts in Literary Forms

Ronald J. Pelias

SENSE PUBLISHERS
ROTTERDAM/BOSTON/TAIPEI

A C.I.P. record for this book is available from the Library of Congress.

ISBN: 978-94-6300-454-1 (paperback)
ISBN: 978-94-6300-455-8 (hardback)
ISBN: 978-94-6300-456-5 (e-book)

Published by: Sense Publishers,
P.O. Box 21858,
3001 AW Rotterdam,
The Netherlands
https://www.sensepublishers.com/

All chapters in this book have undergone peer review.

Printed on acid-free paper

All Rights Reserved © 2016 Sense Publishers

No part of this work may be reproduced, stored in a retrieval system, or transmitted in any form or by any means, electronic, mechanical, photocopying, microfilming, recording or otherwise, without written permission from the Publisher, with the exception of any material supplied specifically for the purpose of being entered and executed on a computer system, for exclusive use by the purchaser of the work.

PRAISE FOR
IF THE TRUTH BE TOLD

"In this remarkable new work Ron Pelias offers us touching, lyrical accounts of both the profound and the everyday. Indeed, the joy of *If the Truth Be Told* is how Pelias conveys these simultaneously, the one through the other: the intensity in the mundane, the ordinary in the complex. Through the detailed attention he gives to both content and form—his discerning observational eye and his keen grasp of the intricacies of literary form and voice—he takes us into the range of human experience: from the ache and loss of ageing to bitter-sweet childhood episodes, from the strains and refrains of domestic relating to questions of faith and belief, from horror to sadness to laughter to love, and more. We accompany him into the universality of our little lives and he leaves us somewhere other than where we were. The book is a joy. Read, write, teach, live."
– Jonathan Wyatt, Edinburgh University

"If the truth be told, I'd say that Ron Pelias recognizes and shows readers that truth is a slippery subject. Using poems, plays, stories, monologues, short dramas, and essays, he provides a vision of truth-telling as a caring, humane, and ethically demanding quest as well as a shifting, illusive, and sometimes frustrating struggle. Blending fiction and nonfiction, personal narratives and newspaper accounts, and autoethnography and ethnography, Pelias creates literary texts that eloquently represent the quandaries of childhood, religion, violence, relationships, aging, retirement, illness, death, and telling truths. In the process, Pelias becomes a conversational partner for the reader, modeling a perceptive, introspective, and caring manner of coping with the challenges of truth-telling through the life cycle. If the truth be told, I'd confess that I found myself in many of the stories he told; I anticipate that other readers will as well, and we'll all be better for it. *If the Truth Be Told* solidifies Pelias's standing as a wise and creative writer par excellence."
– Carolyn Ellis, University of South Florida

"If the truth be told, I think everyone should read this book. Pelias glides so easily back and forth, between poetry and prose, between memory and imagination, between his (genuine) gentle heart and his (imagined) criminal mind, between essay and parody, between script and quip, between loving us all with the light that shines forth from our depths and skewering us with the darkness that sometimes engulfs our hearts … that we quickly begin to glide with him, to develop a groove, to fall into the rhythm of his words. This is a remarkable book, a human journey that does not weary, though it is at times strenuous. You will not be disappointed. Buy this book. Read it. My bet is that you will want to read it again. And again …"
– Christopher N. Poulos, University of North Carolina at Greensboro

"In conversation when one uses the interjection 'If the truth be told,' it is typically accompanied by an admission of one's true feelings. This interjection rhetorically clears the discursive field to allow the individual to state something that he or she might otherwise not say, or might even lie about in order to be polite or to maintain appearances. Pelias' *If the Truth Be Told* explores the blurry zone between the fictive and the factual implied by this interjection by placing emphasis more on the conjunction 'if' and less on any certain 'truth.' Through an array of writing strategies—poems, micro dramas, monologues, essays, flash fiction, and literary nonfiction—he draws upon his life, others' experiences, and his imagination to put into play a myriad of speaker's perspectives in order to illuminate with deft precision and concision the stakes and challenges in telling any truth. For anyone interested in learning how to poetically and creatively capture the human experience, *If the Truth Be Told* is a must read. Each tale richly satisfies yet whets the desire for more; the only solution is to keep reading right through to the end."
– Lesa Lockford, Bowling Green State University

"Pierced with vivid and vulnerable description, emerging optimism, and inconclusive resolution, Pelias offers an incomparable model of autoethnographic and performative inquiry, as well as a remarkable account of an accomplished life."
– Tony E. Adams, Northeastern Illinois University

TABLE OF CONTENTS

Acknowledgments ... xi

Beginnings: If the Truth Be Told ... xiii

Chapter 1: Relational Logics ... 1

    Wanting ... 1
    Now ... 2
    Performance ... 3
    The Ideal Partner ... 4
    Spitting Together ... 6
    Waiting ... 7
    First Love ... 8
    When I Came Home ... 9
    Mutual Embraces ... 10
    One Night Stand ... 14
    Cruelties ... 15
    Lonely Deer ... 20
    Finis ... 21
    Custody Battle ... 22
    Against ... 24
    Asking ... 25
    Moving ... 26
    Getting It Right ... 27
    Olga ... 29
    Another Year ... 30

Chapter 2: Childhood and Adolescent Dangers ... 35

    Starbucks ... 35
    Suffocating ... 37
    Bookcase ... 39
    Curiosity ... 43
    Toddler Found in Schoolyard ... 45

TABLE OF CONTENTS

 Boy   46
 Long Range   48
 Childhood Distress   49
 Don't   53
 Dead Man's Alley   54
 Bobby   57
 Back Yard   58
 School Instruction   59
 Manacle Mom   65
 Fifteen High School Micro-Dramas   67
 Stuck   70
 Drinking   71
 In Search of a Drinking Song   73

Chapter 3: Jesus Chronicles   75

 For the Children   75
 Kudzu Communion   76
 No More   77
 Church Going   78
 Christian Spinoffs   82
 Body to Body   83
 Judgment   84
 Priest Confesses   85
 Following God's Law   87
 A Christian Education   88
 Prayers   91
 The Trick   95
 You Can't Boo Jesus   97

Chapter 4: Criminal Tales   101

 The Drugstore Heist   101
 Woman Charged   105
 Man Ordered   106
 The Interview   108
 The Criminal Mind   115
 From the Bridge   117

Railway Shooting	118
Crimes of United States Politicians	119
Twin	122
Shotgun Murder	123
Ruined Day	124
An Open Letter to the Person Who Broke into My House	125
Painted Body Parts	127
On the One-Year Anniversary of Ferguson	128
Staying Inside	132
Last Words	134
When Those We Call Great Fall	135
Chapter 5: Aging, Illness, and Death Lessons	**139**
The Worry List	139
Surfaces	141
Woman Hospitalized	142
On Going Nuts	143
Going Home	145
When	146
The End of an Academic Career	148
Still Waiting	160
How to Watch Your Mother Die	161
Old Bones	162
Cremation Endings	163
Morgue	165
Bien	166
Still There	167
Ritual	168
Passing	169
The Grave	170
Always Becoming	171
Chapter 6: Telling Truths	**175**
American Beauty	175
Ken Doll Turns Forty	176
Playing the Game	177

TABLE OF CONTENTS

The Lies Couples Keep	179
Nailed Down	181
On the Streets	182
Neighbor	183
The Teacher	184
Border Crossing	185
Helen	187
Pilot Partly Sucked Out of Airliner	188
Pit Bulls	190
Spills	191
No Rhyme or Reason	192
Old Bald Men	193
How the World Breaks	194
Tell Me the Truth	195
Clues to the Possibility of Hearing the Truth	200
Tears	201
Repair	203
He	204
The Truth	205
A Final Truth	209
Appendix A: An Accounting by Genre of the Author's Truth Telling	211
Appendix B: Engagements	217
Suggested Reading	223
About the Author	227

ACKNOWLEDGMENTS

The pieces listed below have appeared, some in altered form, in the following journals:

"When I Came Home," *Cedar Rock* 2 (Spring 1977): 13; "He," *Tributary* 4 (Winter 1991): 17; "Going Home," *Skylark* (1994): 50; "Border Crossing," *San Fernando Poetry Journal* 14 (1996): 6–7; "Asking," *Baybury Review* 3 (1999): 22; "Pit Bulls," *Rockhurst Review* 14 (2001): 51; "Olga," *Out of Line* (2003): 80; "Old Bones" and "Neighbor," *The Blind Man's Rainbow* 10 (Fall 2004): 2; "Morgue," *Main Street Rag* 11 (Spring 2006): 76; "Spills" and "Starbucks," *Timber Creek Review*, 13 (Spring 2007): 28, 54; "Performance," "Ruined Day," and "Woman Hospitalized," *Margie* 6 (2007): 271–273; "Ken Doll Turns Forty," *Words of Wisdom* 25 (2007): 8; "When Those We Call Great Fall," *Cultural Studies↔Critical Methodologies*, 12.4 (2012): 383–384; "Woman Charged" and "Railway Shooting," *Carnival Literary Magazine*, (2014): 6, 48. http://www.carnivalitmag.com/wp-content/uploads/2014/12/jealousy.pdf; "Bien," *Carcinogenic Poetry*. (2015): www.carcinogenicpoetry.com. (May 2, 2015); "Judgment," *The Café Review*, 26 (Summer 2015): 40; "For the Children," *Slab Literary Magazine*, 10 (2015): 141–142; "Kudzu Communion," *Falling Star Magazine*, (2015); "The End of an Academic Career: The Desperate Attempt to Hang On and Let Go," *Qualitative Inquiry* (2016): 25–29.

BEGINNINGS

If the Truth Be Told

PART 1

If the truth be told, I'd say this book plays with the sense of truth. It's composed of six chapters, "Relational Logics," "Childhood and Adolescent Dangers," "Jesus Chronicles," "Criminal Tales," "Aging, Illness, and Death Lessons," and "Telling Truths." Each chapter includes fictional and nonfictional accounts, including poems, stories, monologues, short dramas, essays, creative nonfiction, and mixed genres, to address each chapter's subject. Some entries are based on my life experiences. Other pieces emerge from newspaper accounts where I keep relatively close to the facts as reported or take great liberty as I allow the newspaper article to serve simply as a trigger for creating a fictional world. Still others are pure inventions, fictional texts that are located in my understanding of what might be true to life.

Moving through the book from beginning to end, you may or may not know whether you are reading a nonfictional or fictional text. Often when encountering a lyric poem, for example, you most likely would assume that the author is sharing his or her feelings; or, to offer another case, when listening to a play, you would typical believe that the dialogue from a play is a fictional exchange between two or more characters. I intentionally subvert such assumptions in this book. Sometimes lyric poems spoken in the first person are fictional and sometimes dramatic texts are real life interactions by nonfictional speakers. My intent in doing so is not to subvert just for the sake of subversion. Instead, I hope to blur the boundaries of what counts as evidence, what might be accepted as truth, what might be of use in everyday lives. In other words, I invite you to consider what you value and why. For me, the driving question of the book is not what really happened (although I provide answers to that concern in Appendix A), but if a given text or chapter is useful to reinforce or alter how you and I might see the world.

If the truth be told, I'd say this book is organized around specific topics in order to create through literary forms a feel for the various subjects. Each chapter can be read from a communicative, psychological, sociological, or cultural perspective that offers a thematic, but not exhaustive, rendering of its subject. I do not include a summary explication abstracted from the literary works. I want the texts to stand on their own, available to you, as literary texts would be, for your own cognitive and affective use. My goal, then, is to present literary works that are effective aesthetically and contribute to an understanding of the chapter's topic. I want you to meet each piece as an individual literary text and as a part of a larger thematic case. Although I have spent considerable time deciding upon the arrangement of the entries for their best effect, I'd also say that the book, similar to a book of poems, can be read in a random order. Each piece has the obligation to stand on its own, both as a literary work and as a note in a thematic case.

If the truth be told, I'd say that this book is methodologically informed by ethnography, autoethnography, poetic and narrative inquiry, and performative writing. Each of these methods shares in common a reliance upon detailed and complex literary accounts as fundamental to their process. Rather than privileging abstracted, generalized findings, these methods trust in the evocative. The literary, as writers and readers have long recognized, has the power to reveal insights into human nature that come to us as recognizable and sometimes as previously unacknowledged truths. These methods also trust in the imaginative, in the possibility that individuals can deeply delve into their own and others' life experiences. In this sense, I might best characterize these methods as imaginative inquiry. They ask for empathy, immersion, and embodiment.

    I have intentionally avoided using citations, including in this chapter where turning to others' previous work might seem more appropriate. I have several reasons for doing so. First, I do not want to resort to selected quotes to support this effort; instead, I rely on the literary texts to serve as evidence for the case I'm making. Second, citation often comes forward as an authoritative source, one that makes a bid as a settled truth. I want to keep the question of truth in play. Third, forgoing citations participates in this book's push against academic conventions, against what counts as evidence, against privileged notions of data. Even so, I bow to academic tradition by including one traditional autoethnographic essay, "The End of An Academic Career," that calls upon citation and by providing an informing bibliography at the end of this book. I hope if you are a reader who could care less about such matters, you will feel free to skip my nods toward academic discourse.

If the truth be told, I'd say that this book can be put to a variety of uses. First, I hope you will read this book for the pleasures that literature can bring. Allow yourself the space to enjoy what's included, although I'm sure you will find some texts more to your liking than others. May some texts encourage you to linger, to pause, cognitively and affectively, as you take in what you've read, and may you feel you've spent your time well after you're finished reading.

For those of you who are teachers, I hope you will feel that this book contributes to discussions of qualitative methods, particularly in regard to what counts as evidence and truth telling, how far qualitative research can be pushed, and what ethical responsibilities researchers might have in relation to truthfulness. Similarly, I hope you find that it adds an implicit communicative, psychological, sociological, and cultural commentary on its respective subjects. That being said, I think the book could work well in qualitative inquiry classes or in communication, psychology, sociology, and cultural studies courses that address any of the included themes. The entries could also be used as a springboard for further inquiry. See Appendix B for a list of possible discussion questions.

PART 2

If the truth be told, I'd say I don't always know what the truth is. Take, for example, the following:

> I retired after thirty-two years from Southern Illinois University because I was worn down, tired fighting students who wanted to

be licensed, but could care less if they learned anything; drained by an administration that appeared much more interested in establishing a record of change so that they might move on to the next overpaid administrative position than in what was happening with or to students; and sapped by over-worked colleagues who felt exploited, and as a result, gave up, refused to do what needed to be done.

I retired after thirty-two years from Southern Illinois University because it didn't make economic sense to stay. The last two years I worked for just about nothing—I would have made close to an equal amount from my pension without doing a thing.

I retired after thirty-two years from Southern Illinois University because I thought it was time. I didn't have the energy for the job that I once had. I was having trouble hearing my students in the classroom. I was less driven to keep up with the literature in my field. I was losing faith in the importance of academic writing. I was allowing myself to use old notes for classes. I felt less joy while doing my job. I started to dread working with another graduate student. I thought if I had to change "their" for "there" on one more of their papers, I'd scream.

I retired after thirty-two years from Southern Illinois University because I thought that is what I wanted, but every day I miss the excitement of the classroom, the daily exchanges with colleagues, the desire and commitment to make the department a place where students and faculty want to be. I miss going to my office, leaving the door open, being ready for the students who might come by. I miss the classroom challenges, always feeling the promise of each new class.

I retired after thirty-two years from Southern Illinois University because I wanted more time to write. A permanent sabbatical seemed wonderfully seductive: Nothing to do, but to get up each morning and write. Finish projects I've been wanting to do. Write more poems, more short stories, perhaps a few plays. What a luxury!

I retired after thirty-two years from Southern Illinois University because my wife had retired a few years before and we were ready to move to on, to live in a larger city, to live closer to my family. My mother wasn't doing well and I wanted to spend more time with her, take some of the burden off my brother and sister.

I've heard all of the above versions come out of my mouth and each time I felt I was telling the truth, explaining to myself and others with as much honesty as I could muster in that moment why I retired. As I write this, it's been more than two years since I walked away from Southern Illinois University, and I am still searching for a narrative that feels settled, that takes away the unease I feel when speaking about my retirement decision. This unease comes because when I try to tell the truth, everything and nothing I say captures what feels true to me. This unease at times drives me to add a tag to a version I might be sharing: "That's how I make sense of it *today*."

If the truth be told, I'd say the truth can never be told. Perhaps I overstate the case. I do believe I cannot walk through solid walls without some new transformative power, leap from a tall building without injury, or stay under water for an extended period of time without consequences, although I do not test these possibilities everyday, and I take for granted that there are such things as walls, tall buildings, and water. Some things appear to me as aspects of material reality that I am well-served to accept as true. Such obdurate facts seem to transcend linguistic and social construction. I am glad, however, that what people have taken as unquestionable has been questioned and, at times, proven wrong. To get through my day, though, I function as if such things are reality. I trust, for better or worse, some things are true, real.

I am equally sure that no matter what story I might tell, I could tell it another way. I could add, for instance, the word "long" to modify "years" in the repeated phrase at the start of each version of my retirement stories, and I would have changed the meaning, made my time at Southern Illinois University appear more burdensome. I could offer new details, elaborate or minimize perspectives, include others' versions, and so on. Each possibility opens up alternative ways of making sense, of telling the truth.

As time passes, I am likely to alter my retirement stories. I might forget some things, might bury some of my experiences. Writing my retirement stories now, my desire is to include all the relevant stories, but I am not sure if I'm remembering every version I've shared with myself and others. Time might influence what seems more or less important to me. For example, the antipathy I feel toward the administration I left behind at Southern Illinois University might dissipate, seem less relevant. I might, if I were to revise these pages at a later date, change how I would present that. Time might also lead me to adjust my narratives to meet the needs of a specific moment. Using my retirement accounts for the purposes of this discussion, I select stories that help me make the points I'm trying to put forward, but if I were writing for a different purpose at a different time, I might make a different decision about how to present these tales. Now and in the future, I will and will not believe that I am telling the truth.

I know, too, that whatever story I share is in part a product of my individual characteristics and cultural context, that if my same experiences had been lived by someone else from some other cultural framework, the stories that would emerge would be different. Bound by language, time, and culture, my stories take form and reflect the truth as I see it. I cannot escape myself.

Sometimes when I think I am telling the truth, I am aware that my stories change because the version I am sharing takes into account my audience. I most often give the economic explanation to people who I don't know well and who are not participants in academic life. Some of the accounts I share only with close friends, ones who I trust would be open to my feelings during this life transition. Some I offer as official statements to students or administrators. As I speak with different people about my retirement, I make assessments about the appropriateness of details, levels of personal disclosure, and the constraints of relational history. In other words, the truth I share becomes audience dependent.

If the truth be told, I'd say I always know when I'm intentionally telling a lie. I believe I am trying my best to tell you the truth as I see it, and given the cautionary notes I've describe above, I stand by the honesty of my account. What I've written seems true to my experience, seems like I'm sharing with you with as much openness as I can what I believe. If I told you that I had been looking forward to retirement for the last twenty years, I would be lying. That simply is not true to my experience. I would view such a statement as a lie, and I try not to lie in my daily life, although I must admit that I have lied. When I have spoken dishonestly, I feel it as an interpersonal breach, a betrayal of trust, a stone sitting in my stomach, sometimes consequential and sometimes not. I may in such situations try to justify my lie, but I cannot escape my sense that I failed to tell the truth.

Knowing what is and what isn't a lie often is not as clear cut as the above paragraph might suggest. Sometimes what I say reflects shades of truth, i.e., exaggerations, eliminations, misrepresentations, and so on. In such cases, my intent serves as my guide to my sense of lying or truth telling. In the retirement stories I've shared above, I did not mention that after moving to Lafayette I took a part-time teaching position at the University of Louisiana. To say I've retired is a bit misleading, but my intent was not to hide that detail. It just did not emerge in the telling of those stories. This does not feel like a lie to me. On the other hand, I've said to others that I was playing a lot of golf when asked if that was how I was spending my retirement days. The truth is that I've played some, but not nearly as much as I thought I would. Answering in the affirmative seemed the easiest response. To explain why I haven't played more golf seemed more than I wanted to share at that time and my intent was to truncate the conversation by allowing their assumption to stand. In short, I answered with a lie. Intent, in my scheme of personal truth telling, matters.

My sense of truth telling is not the only assessment that matters. Those who take in my words also make a judgment. Typically, people assume others are telling the truth unless they have some reason to question the speaker's account. I try to honor that social contract, to be an honest person in my interactions with others. I feel that burden not only in my personal life, but also when I am writing with a scholarly or literary form that readers expect to be true to the writer's experience. When writing an autoethnographic account, for example, I feel that if I were to deliberately lie, I would be diminishing the power of what I have to offer. When I write a memoir, I don't want to suffer the consequences of the writers who have told falsehoods in their life stories. I want my writing to be trustworthy, honestly rendered.

If the truth be told, then, I'd say the truth is elusive, contingent, difficult to nail down, but when spoken, always does or does not carry a personal sense of veracity.

PART 3

If the truth be told, I'd say writing this book was both joyous and distressing. Little is more satisfying for writers than to see their work come into form, to reach a sense of completion. Because so many of the pieces in this book are short, I had the joyous pleasure of feeling I'd written a text to my satisfaction over and over again. A smile would cross my face, I'd print the pages, and I'd hold the piece in my hands as if it were a sacred text. Such moments are glorious, but, of course, they do not last. The next time I'd read a piece that seemed so satisfying, I'd feel like it should be put in the trash, that I should start over. Sometimes I would discard it and begin again, and sometimes I'd revise, trying to find what might make the piece better. It can be a never-ending process, but, like most writers, I reach the point where I'm willing to release my work for publication, even though I'm not confident it is ready for others' eyes. That's part of the stress of putting words to the page.

Writing this book has filled me with doubts. I am an academic by trade, not a creative writer. Although I've taken a few creative writing classes, attended writing workshops over the years, been writing poems since my high school sweetheart fell for someone else, published a number of poems in small literary journals, and have an educational background in the performance of literature, I've never felt licensed as a writer, never became a member of the writing community, never thought I had permission to call myself a writer. I'm not sure who I thought might one day wave a magic wand over my head and say, "You are a writer now." When I retired, I considered returning to school for a MFA in creative writing, but that has not happened. Perhaps if I got a MFA, I might feel like I could embrace that label, "writer," might know who might wave the wand. But I suspect I'll never apply to a creative writing program, never take that step. So here I am, putting forward words that I am calling literary and I am filled with doubts.

I have a friend who believes that he became a writer once he allowed himself to apply that label to himself. For him, considering himself a writer was enabling. I have always felt just the opposite. Calling myself a writer had the effect of freezing me in front of a blank page. I would write poems, stories, and plays as a hobby, but I've never called myself a creative writer, until now. It was one thing for me to flirt with the literary when I was writing as a scholar, but it is quite another to write as if my texts merit literary attention. I write now with that intention and, quite honestly, it adds to my concern as I put this book out for your consideration. It has also been a wonderful joy and an exciting challenge that for the first time has felt productive for me.

If the truth be told, I'd say writing this book, as well as other books I've written, is simultaneously the most selfish and selfless thing I do. To write a book means you will spend countless hours in front of your computer or in what might be called "solitary refinement." You will resent others when you are interrupted, particularly if words are coming quickly. You will ignore those you love, ask more of them than you should. You will find your mind drifting to the next section of your book when you should be paying attention to others. You will be grumpy when you are struggling to find how a piece might work. Mood swings will become your normal way of being. You will think you're clever and smart as well as simplistic and dumb as an old shoe. You will believe your work is more important than it really is. You will perceive yourself as an artist and as a fifth-rate hack. You will be needy. You will be hard to live with.

At same time, you will feel you're making sacrifices, giving yourself over to a higher calling, creating something that might be useful, open possibilities, further dialogue. You will see how your work stands alongside the work of others. You will trust that it is a contribution. You will put aside feelings that your efforts are irrelevant, a waste of paper and ink. You will push on, believing in the worth of your labor, even on days when you'd rather be doing anything else. You will see yourself as part of a larger community's calling, doing what is expected and valued. You will forfeit daily pleasures. Your back will ache; you will not get the exercise you should; you will eat poorly, all in the name of the value of words. You will reject notions that words do little to change the world. You will be an advocate for their power. You will see their influence moving beyond you. You will enjoy how they find their way.

If the truth be told, I'd say writing this book would not have been completed without the help of others. My wife, Mimi Hinchcliff Pelias (University of Louisiana), continues to serve as a wonderful conversational partner and as a superb editor. Her thoughtful presence is a safety net against my stupidity. Tony E. Adams (Northeastern Illinois University), Carolyn Ellis (University of South Florida), Lesa Lockford (Bowling Green State University), Christopher N. Poulos (University of North Carolina, Greensboro), and Jonathan Wyatt (The University of Edinburgh) have graciously given of their time and critical insights to make this book a better read. Patricia Leavy, the editor of the Social Fictions Series for Sense Publishers, went well beyond what any author might expect in bringing a book to publication. I cannot imagine having a better working relationship with an editor. Thank you, Patricia, for your time, for your insights, and for your professionalism.

PART 4

If the truth be told, I'd say the truth does not equal the sum of its parts.

CHAPTER 1

RELATIONAL LOGICS

WANTING

She wanted him to write her a love poem, one better than anyone had ever written. She said it should be filled with how beautiful their love is, how it carries them. He said words are just words—it's actions that matter and he offered her his hand. She took it, but insisted that words have a power that actions don't and whispered in his ear that she loved him. He smiled and kissed her cheek, feeling their love so strongly that he began to cry. "I'm sorry," he said, trying to contain himself. "Yes, yes, yes," she replied, feeling the presence of their poem.

CHAPTER 1

NOW

In the large room
once not large enough
need now only hold one sofa
where we sit,

always touching, where
our legs intertwine,
where the cats struggle
to find their place.

On the brown pillows,
our heads now turn
toward our smiles
lighting the large room.

In such light
history is mere history
and now is forever
in this large room.

PERFORMANCE

Jayde Hanson,
knife thrower extraordinaire,
the best ever
to twirl a blade
through the air,
appeared
on live TV
with his girlfriend, Yana,
always so still,
who watched the knives
dive into the hard wood,
sticking by her side,
slipping between her legs,
sliding by her neck.
He was showing how many knives
he could hurl in one minute
when one came a little low,
sliced her head.
The blood oozed.
He said it was only a nick.
Apologies were made.
Yana is now concentrating
on her hula-hoop act.
He is looking for a new assistant,
a new girlfriend,
one less prone to outburst.

CHAPTER 1

THE IDEAL PARTNER

Hands that move with ease, sometimes as free as a butterfly's flutter and sometimes as determined as a dog digging up a bone, punctuating talk, saying more than words; that know when to take mine, squeezing tight to claim our connection, to say I'm with you in this moment of need, to insist we stand together against whatever might come our way; that rest on my thigh with a comfortable familiarity, like a cat settling down, claiming space, claiming here, here is where I belong.

Fingers that intertwine with mine, locking us together as we walk or sit watching a film, pulling us closer like the laces on a shoe; that come toward me, extended, ready, rushing toward touch; that do not recoil from the intimacy of the splinter, of the wound; that massage my back, run through my hair, draw circles, figure eights, and sliding snakes on my chest or arm.

Feet that know when to come close and when to move away; that welcome being washed, rubbed with lotion, being cradled in my lap; that, depending on the terrain, dance or stumble through the day, marking what to kick aside and what not to trample, returning to me, to where we stand face-to-face, each foot beside another foot.

Body that wants to be with mine, snuggles in tight, slips next to me like honey into a jar; that moves unashamed, recognizes its flaws and laughs; that is ready for the painter's eye, its curves finding the shadows and the light; that bends into intimacy, a leaning in, a head on a shoulder, a back against my chest; that knows its desires; that releases its weight, body to body, in the moment after.

Hair, long or short, light or dark, that invites a breathing in, its smell delicate and fresh; that carries the sun and peeks underneath hats; that knows its style without looking fixed; that separates between my fingers like gathered silk threads.

Mouth that is quick to smile, to laugh, its teeth revealing themselves, its lips thin as a whisper or full as a shout turning up to greet me, its tongue peeking out, slipping back in, sliding by mine; that chews on what troubles and understands what to and what not to swallow; that opens to air its views, speaking with conviction, with compassion, with consideration.

Eyes that look, deeply, linger as they meet mine; that stare through the dark and blink against the deceptive light; that tell the truth and expose the hidden; that measure, hold me accountable; that keep me in my place, sometimes pushing me away, sometimes pulling me in; that are quick to soften.

Ears that turn to my sounds, to take in my most mundane and most profound as if both were worth hearing; that sit eye level, its intricate curves echoing what needs repetition and blocking what needs to be forgotten; that channels my whispers into the heard, alert when I might whimper.

CHAPTER 1

SPITTING TOGETHER

We didn't know anything about cherry pit spitting until we went to our county fair and saw this table where you could enter this contest. Rick said, "I think I'll try it. It's only two bucks and you can win all those prizes." There was a big stuffed giraffe, tickets to the stock car races that night, and a bunch other little things. That first time Rick tried it, he came in second and we got some stuff. Not bad, uh? Well, Rick found out about other contests and we started traveling together. Before you know it, we were married and Rick had me spitting too. He'd be against the men and I'd be against the women. We bought a motorcycle and we would go from place to place, mostly on the weekends, so we could participate. Pretty soon, we were the top contenders. I don't want to brag or anything, but Rick has won nine international championships now and I've won five.

Rick's a real showman. He likes to ride in on his motorcycle, drop to his knees in the spitter's box, and let it fly. He usually sends them over fifty feet, enough to win most of the time.

Against the woman, thirty or thirty-five feet will usually win. For a good spit, the trick is how you control your breath and how you fix your tongue. Rick taught me that.

What I really wanted to tell you, though, is that spitting together is what makes our marriage work. Spitting brought us together and it keeps us together. I know that might sound funny or weird, but, like they say, you need something in common to make a marriage work. We got cherry pit spitting. When we are on the road, my arms wrapped around my Rick, life can't be any better. And when we win, well, that's icing on the cake.

WAITING

Waiting,
waiting for you.

The rain comes,
lightly at first,

then harder
and harder.

I wait
through the rain,

through the silence
of the room

for your knock.
The phone rings,

startles—
no one is there.

I wait,
a candle

burning,
flickering, until

you never come.

CHAPTER 1

FIRST LOVE

You never forget, they say, how, after all the years, your first love will still come back, her teenage image imprinted; how she still holds part of you in the world of "what if," what if you hadn't gone away to school, what if you'd told her…, what if she loved you how you loved her; how your love for her became lifelong instruction on what you should feel, should know, in your heart before you commit, showing you, over and over again, how rare it is to truly love; how you dismiss your own arguments that you were too young or too naïve to know what love is; how on the night before you left for school, she let you touch her breasts, and you felt it was the most sacred moment you've ever experienced; how she lingers and lingers in your head; how you wish you had never sent her those poems since you learned from your first-year English teacher that the poems, while heartfelt, were not very good, and she was always better in English than you were, and she probably knew right away that they weren't very good, and that's why she broke it off with you, broke it off so she could date your friend, Butch, who was always a better athlete than you were; and you remember that even though she was perfect, how she could act like a bitch, like when she decided to come to summer school where you were going and you were so excited that she agreed to do that, but when she got there, she just started dating other people, and you were broken hearted again; how years later you tracked her down and you met her for coffee, but you could tell, after about ten minutes, that she wasn't very interested in you or your life, and she just wanted to get away from you, but, instead, she pity fucked you and you were happy, but mostly sad, and your heart broke just a little more; and how, even now, after all that, you still love her.

WHEN I CAME HOME

I found you bathing in oil,
shining like sweat,
as I sat at your side
the steam slid up,
hot and wet.

Water rocked against your breasts
and with each slight wave,
my eyes held you
as you soaked off the smell
of your other lover.

CHAPTER 1

MUTUAL EMBRACES

Mutual embraces pull us together to celebrate, to support, and to show affection. We step forward, calling upon our bodies to connect, to open ourselves, a body welcoming another body, arms encircling, hands and fingers pressing in, saying, at least for this moment, we will take each other in, stand together in this act of public or private acknowledgment, in this shared behavior of telling affect.

What Embraces Accomplish

Mutual embraces pull you to others in celebration,
> like when you are greeted by a friend or family member after you have been away, telling you that presence and absence matters, that you have a meaningful place in each other's life;

> like when you mark your victory on the playing field, recognizing what you all accomplished together, what it means to be a part of something larger than yourself, and you find yourself hugging everyone, everyone at the same time;

> like when you complete a difficult job, knowing what it took, the costs, the labor, the results, believing only those of you who were a part could understand;

> like when you participate in ceremonial congratulations—the wedding line, the high school or college graduation, the initiation, the religious rite—to applaud a transition, an earned movement toward the promise of a better future.

Mutual embraces pull you to others in support,
> like when you take a frightened child into your arms and say, "It will be alright. Don't worry. I've got you now," and the child begins to feel safe, protected by your engulfing arms;

> like when you are experiencing some personal difficulty—a betrayal, a job loss, money problems—trying to get through it, trying to face what is behind and what is ahead, and you find that a hug from a friend, family member, or partner has

more power than a solution, that being held offers strength and needed comfort;

like when you are facing an illness and you feel so alone and a hug says, "I'm right here with you, ready to help in any way I can," and your sobs wet the other's shirt, and you can breathe just a bit more easily;

like when you have no words, like in times of loss, that can be a cure, no words that can truly soothe, that can alleviate the pain, when touch is what heals.

Mutual embraces pull you to others in affection,

like when you are welcomed because you stepped forward, stepped into a situation by choice, by affiliation, by a nodding toward the other who acknowledges your gesture with inviting open arms;

like when you take a casual, momentary pause to connect, to acknowledge that you care; a brief contact that serves as a means of checking in, of asking if everything is alright, of saying I want you to remember that I love you;

like when you mark a long shared history, an intimacy earned and cherished, that allows joyous and difficult memories to rush back as you stand there knowing that the bond between the two of you has not and will never be broken;

like when an intense experience—being robbed at gunpoint, climbing to the mountain's top, surviving an accident— reminds you of your own mortality and you commemorate your continued existence by taking life into your arms;

like when you ask for forgiveness and the forgiver initiates contact telling you that your transgression will be, if not forgotten, put aside, and you feel yourself breathing again, taking in the smell of the person you love;

like when you find your way into intimacy and the moment feels seductive—when two bodies push against each other

CHAPTER 1

during a slow dance or deep kiss, or when you linger in each other arms not wanting to separate, to be apart, or when you make love and you can't hold the person you love tight enough.

How Embraces Are Performed

Mutual embraces call upon your body to touch,

with a step forward, positioning your body in relation to another's, most often with feet between feet; with a tilt forward at the waist so that only arms and cheeks might touch or with full body to full body contact; with arms gently and safely placed to signal no sexual intent or arms wrapped around, holding each other firmly to indicate a deep connection; with hands still or hands moving up and down, perhaps offering a slight pat or perhaps pressing down gently;

with limited or extended duration, depending upon your sensitivity or insensitivity to the bodily cues sent from one body to the other that suggest when you should release or linger; depending upon the relationship between the participating individuals; depending upon context, whether it's public or private, it's with a group or alone, it's socially and culturally sanctioned;

with caution, moving slowly, trying to read what seems right, trying to decide just what to do, taking hints, sensing just how far to go, most often erring on the side of less rather than more to demonstrate respect, or with abandon, rushing in, pulling each other closer and closer, wanting the contact, wanting to be there, wanting to fall into each other.

How Embraces Feel

Mutual embraces make you feel connected,

as if you're tied together, tightly, knotted by the pleasures of contact, of flesh meeting flesh; emotionally linked, filling you with warmth as your body smiles, filling you with what you understand as love;

as if you're physically trapped, coerced to do what you'd rather not, held against your better judgment and your unspoken wishes, in a place where escape carries larger consequences than completing the gesture, making you feel helpless, used, and, perhaps, dirty.

Mutual embraces make you feel evaluated,
> as if you were told you are desired, belong in relation to others, allowing you to define yourself by their presence, their willingness to place their bodies next to yours and to hold you, making you feel endorsed, making you believe that you might matter to someone besides yourself;
>
> as if eyes are watching you, measuring you, telling you where you stand, that you've done something wrong, suggesting that desires do not have equal intents, making you feel embarrassed, awkward, inappropriate, taken apart.

Mutual embraces make you feel loved,
> as if your bodies found a home, a private place where you can breathe in, become one, elevated beyond bodily limit, merged together by the muscle of your affection, by the hum of two bodies giving, each to each.

CHAPTER 1

ONE NIGHT STAND

The raucous laughter from the night before
gives way to the wide window morning.
The day starts as if it were already a chore
to watch the alarming sun, slowly rising,

they yawn, mouths stale as smoke,
move by empty bottles and bent cans
before the air meets some half-witted joke.
Seasoned veterans, always making plans,

sharp at night, stained in daylight.
Both prisoner and guard with mocking faces
in cadenced terror of each other's sight
have found their hard and private places.

CRUELTIES

1.

Partner 1: Are you really planning to go out looking like that?
Partner 2: What's wrong with how I look?
Partner 1: If you don't know, you're beyond help.
Partner 2: I think I look fine.
Partner 1: If that's what you want to believe, fine.

2.

Person 1: What if I were to ask you out?
Person 2: Are you planning on doing that?
Person 1: What if I said let's go to dinner and then to a film next Friday?
Person 2: Next Friday?
Person 1: Yes, next Friday. Does that work for you?
Person 2: Never works for me.

3.

Partner 1: You wouldn't believe what he did the other night.
Partner 2: Do you have to tell everything that happens in our house?
Partner 1: It's funny. I never saw anything like it before.
Partner 2: I had the flu.
Partner 1: Yeah, he had the flu and he starts throwing up in the toilet, and as he was throwing up, he shits all over himself. There he was throwing up and shit coming out all over. It was quite a sight.
Partner 2: I had the flu.
Partner 1: I'll have that image in my head forever. You should have seen him. He was a mess. Shit running down his leg. His head in the toilet.

CHAPTER 1

4.

Friend 1: You won't believe what Ted said about you. Said he didn't think you could handle the job. Said it right there in the meeting with Mr. Franks.
Friend 2: Ted said that?
Friend 1: Yeah. And he claims to be your friend. What kind of friend is that?
Friend 2 Ted really said that?
Friend 1: Yeah. I thought you'd want to know.

5.

Partner 1: How many times do I have to say I'm sorry?
Partner 2: Until I believe you. Until I can find a way to forgive you.
Partner 1: It's been two years.
Partner 2: I still live with it every day. I wake up and that's what I think about.
Partner 1: You need to let it go.
Partner 2: I can't.
Partner 1: You mean you won't.
Partner 2: Don't you think I would leave this behind if I could?
Partner 1: I think you like holding it over me.
Partner 2: I can't believe you said that. Just leave me alone. Get away from me.

6.

Friend 1: You didn't know that? What an idiot!
Friend 2: I guess I just forgot.
Friend 1: No, you just didn't know it. You dumb fuck.

7.

Partner 1: You need to do what I tell you to do.
Partner 2: What if I don't?

Partner 1: You'll be sorry. Real sorry.
Partner 2: You always making your threats, but you're not man enough to do anything. I'll go out if I want.
Partner 1: Don't push me.
Partner 2: I'm out of here.
Partner 1: I'm warning you! I'm warning you!
Partner 2: Bye.

8.

Partner 1: We can get married now.
Partner 2: Now that we can, I'm not sure if I still want to marry you.
Partner 1: What do you mean?
Partner 2: Let me say it straight: I don't want to marry you.
Partner 1: How long have you felt this way?
Partner 2: Since I've known you.

9.

Friend 1: I can't believe you did that.
Friend 2: What do you mean? People do that all the time.
Friend 1: Not on a first date.
Friend 2: We both wanted to do it. It felt right.
Friend 1: Well, it's not right.

10.

Partner 1: You bore me.
Partner 2: That's not a very nice thing to say.
Partner 1: I'm just telling you the truth.
Partner 2: Maybe it would be better if you didn't always say the truth.
Partner 1: You want me to lie to you.
Partner 2: I want you to be sensitive.
Partner 1: I tell it like it is.
Partner 2: You tell it so it hurts.

CHAPTER 1

11.

Partner 1: You're no good at anything.
Partner 2: I'm doing good in school.
Partner 1: That's because you go to that community college with all the other dumb kids.
Partner 2: Jenny goes there and she's smart.
Partner 1: You think she's smart. She's as big an idiot as you are.

12.

Partner 1: Please don't bother me with your little hobby.
Partner 2: Writing is not my hobby. It's what I do.
Partner 1: Okay then, please don't bother me with that little thing you do.

13.

Friend 1: I don't know why you like them.
Friend 2: They're sweet.
Friend 1: But they're such nerds.
Friend 2: They're smart and I think they're cute.
Friend 1: If you say so, but I can't see why you would spend time with them.

14.

Friend 1: Say that I'm willing to come over just to fuck, but I don't want to talk or do anything else.
Friend 2: That's mean. I can't say that.
Friend 1: You think it's mean because you're all sensitive and shit. You need to learn how the world works. You have to know what you want.
Friend 2: That's not how I want to be.
Friend 1: That's why you'll always find yourself on the bottom of the pile.

15.

Partner 1: I'd rather masturbate than make love to you.
Partner 2: It takes two to make it work. If you took more time to understand what I need, then it would be better.
Partner 1: You always want to put the blame on me.
Partner 2: Just when it is your fault, and, you have to admit, most of the time it is your fault.
Partner 1: It's my fault that you don't know how to make love.
Partner 2: It's your fault you make me not want to make love to you.

CHAPTER 1

LONELY DEER

I looked at him laughing,
watching that buck
fuck that painted deer,
and I hated him
for all the years
I've been his bedroom
ornament,
cold and still,
silent as he would
pound away
doing his thing,
driven like that buck.
It's not natural
to make metal into flesh
or flesh into metal.
It's not right
not to notice.
So when the buck
trotted off
and he wanted his turn,
I turned away
refusing to be that
ever again.

FINIS

Listening for the possibility of us
I hit the wrong keys. You were clear.
Not now. Not us together. Not ever.

You offer a hug as a teacher might
to the student who can't get it right.
Try again. Diminuendo. Not Crescendo.

Notice the correct hand position.
I was too busy rumbling around
the bottom bass of my poor scales

to hear the dead clink
of your final treble notes.
We are an unplayable score,

broken bars sliding off the page,
the cello's sorrow and the drum's
deep beat: gone, gone.

CHAPTER 1

CUSTODY BATTLE

Things went bad from the start. I only stayed with Liz as long as I did because of Jessica, the only good that came from those five years. Our honeymoon lasted about a day before we knew it was a mistake. It's funny how everything seems perfect until you say, "I do." Then, everything falls like dominoes all in a row. Jessica was going to make things right but, of course, she didn't. She became the rope in our tug-of-war.

I thought I loved Joe when I married him. We had been dating for about a year, and he was always the perfect gentleman. He showed me respect, never forced himself. After we got married, he always wanted to be on me, thought it was his right. I'd let him have his way most of time, but sometimes the thought of him pounding away and collapsing on me with the whole weight of the night was more than I could endure. He knew, but he kept coming until we got Jessica.

We never made love; we only had sex. When we were done, I'd feel like shit. She hated it. You can tell. I tried to make it work, but no matter what I did, she was just waiting until I was done. Once Jessica was born, I stopped asking. It wasn't worth it. I'd rather be with Jessica, holding her, knowing her love from her smile. Even with my two jobs, I spent more time with Jessica than Liz did. She was too busy doing whatever she does in that room of hers. After I'd put Jessica down, I'd hear Liz crying.

It wasn't just the sex. He started bossing me around. At first, it wasn't too bad, but once Jessica was born, I couldn't do anything right. I'd put the diaper on too tight or too loose, feed her too much or too little. I'd even hold her wrong. I couldn't do it anymore. I couldn't take it. I made the spare room my own. When Joe came home, that's where I'd go. Eventually, I moved out. I couldn't take it. That's when my plan took hold—I'd fix him a supper, watch him eat himself out of my life.

I should have known when she asked me to dinner. We were separated, waiting for the court to decide who got Jessica. She's the one who left, left Jessica behind. I thought maybe she'd come to her senses, that we'd be able to talk things through, but the woman is nuts. I should have known when she put that dish down, all smiles. It wasn't like her. I ate a little, but it tasted off. She kept saying, "Eat up." She was getting nervous. When I pushed my plate away, she pulled the gun.

He was saying that no matter what I said, he was going to get Jessica. Said I wasn't capable of caring for her, that I had abandoned her, but it was him I left. He hardly ate anything, going on and on about how I wasn't a fit mother. That smug face of his kept coming across the table, poisoning me. I had the gun to protect myself. I didn't think I'd really have to shoot him. Last I saw him, he was running out the house, holding his shoulder. That was the last time I saw Jessica too.

CHAPTER 1

AGAINST

Against the low morning sky
a blackbird banked,
calling for its mate.
The gray of fall was settling in.
Frost held the browning grass
as the wind slipped by.

Six months ago she left
when spring sat in full promise.
A quiet rain covered the car.
The dandelions, readying themselves,
lifted their heads.
I stood on the porch, watching.

This winter the fence
will probably come down—
the weight of snow being too much.
Too late to bring the plants in.
The best one can do
is start again next year.

ASKING

She asks how I'm feeling
and I report
Without hands or lips
alone
and from the inside
out
as public and private
as a confession

She asks if I ever thought
about taking my life
and I answer
That's all I do
I take it everywhere
like a good Catholic
carrying a rosary
fingering sins

She asks if I remember
my dreams
and I say
My dreams forgot me long ago
when I sleep, I slip
away, down,
to the world
dead

CHAPTER 1

MOVING

The lawn sat up like a welcoming mat
in front of their lovely two-story home.
Flowers seemed to bloom year around.
Inside were plants, two kittens, and a piano
their son was learning to play. Everything
was in order. All seemed right.

He lifts one end of the stripped sofa to carry it
to the open mouth of the U-Haul truck.
Its silver tongue is ready to slide everything in.
He is moving out into a small apartment
with a musty smell, down dark stairs.
As he packs what they decided would be his,
he leave holes, empty spaces
that once were filled with decision,
imprints, set into the rug, of the table,
the love seat, and the bed frame,
known from their years of use.

GETTING IT RIGHT

We're getting it right this time. I know most people would think I'm crazy to be marrying the same woman for the seventh time, but I've got a good idea of what went wrong with the first six times we tied the knot, and I won't make those mistakes again. As I look back, I know that our first marriage didn't last because we were too young—at 18 and 19 you just don't have any sense. We needed to grow up, live a little, before we were ready to settle down. So I admit, I cheated on her, and she was right to kick me out, but that other woman didn't mean anything to me.

It took several years, but she forgave me and we decided to get married for the second time. This time I was faithful. I'd learned my lesson, but after our first two kids came, we seemed to drift apart. She didn't have time for me anymore. I mean, with her job, the house, and all she had to do with the kids, it was like I didn't matter anymore. That was hard for me so I cut out.

We got married for the third time mostly for the kids. I was missing them and I wanted to be a good father to them. She wouldn't marry me again unless I promised to help more with the kids and the house. She said that's why things didn't work for us before, so I promised. I guess I wasn't as good as I should have been in keeping that promise, and we started fighting about this and that. Little things. Nothing serious. But I hated being around all that bickering so I started going to get a few beers after work. Before I knew it, I wasn't getting home until 10:00 or 11:00 at night. That went on for quite a while before she decided she had enough. I came home one night and all my clothes were on the porch and she wouldn't let me in.

I lived alone for several years. Drank way too much. I woke up one morning realizing that if I kept living this way, I'd find my way to an early grave. I wanted a good home life. The kids were growing up and I was missing most of it. I pleaded with her to take me back. At first, she didn't want to have anything to do with me, but I kept begging and begging, and she finally agreed to marry me for the fourth time. I know now why she didn't really want me back. She was seeing Jeff, a guy who works for the oil company. She said it wasn't serious, but she kept on seeing him after we got married again. I didn't know that at first, but when I found out, I had to break it off.

I started drinking more and more. I was living alone again, seeing the kids every now and then. The company I was working for started downsizing and I got downsized right along with it. I was drinking all the time now. Somewhere in there, she and Jeff ended their thing and she came knocking on my door. Said she wanted me back. I don't think she knew what bad shape I was in. I was in no position to say no, so we got married for the fifth time. That one didn't last too long. She couldn't deal with me drinking all the time and not having a job.

I was back on my own again. I faced the fact that I had become an alcoholic. Started going to the meetings and I turned myself around. Got another job, not as good as one I had, but good enough to keep food on the table, particularly once I wasn't buying booze all the time. She saw how I changed when I went to apologize to her for all the things I did wrong while I was drinking. It took a while, but I convinced her that I was sober and that we belonged together. We married for the sixth time.

I'm not sure what went wrong with our sixth marriage. Maybe it was because we had gotten use to living alone. Maybe it was because she didn't like my new AA friends. Maybe it was because we couldn't drop all our history and start fresh again. Whatever the reason, we're beyond that now. We've been working hard so that this time we won't make any mistakes. We've made rules for each other that we are going to follow. And we realized that we wouldn't have gotten married so many times if we didn't really love each other. So, the seventh wedding is on. I don't think I'm crazy. This time we're going to make it right.

OLGA

For forty-four years
we've been married.
Stuck together
through thick and thin.
I was always told
that I wasn't smart, too
dumb to even get jokes,
empty-headed, just
what you'd expect
from a blond. But,
I raised his two daughters
as he watched and
watched us with his
critical eyes and cooked
his every meal covering
every dish with his onions
until he smelled just
like the house. I was
there too when his desire
came up, doing my duty,
pretending it was more.
Now, when I look at his
paralyzed body shriveled up
like a dried carrot, his mouth
always open as if ready to
swallow me whole, my
empty head is filled
with anticipation of his passing.

CHAPTER 1

ANOTHER YEAR

CHARACTERS:

  Ben, male, age 67, married to Sylvia
  Sylvia, female, age 67, married to Ben

SETTING:

  Ben and Sylvia are sitting on a small deck behind their modest suburban home. They have a small table and two glasses of wine between them.

AT RISE:

  Ben lifts his wine glass to toast their forty-seventh wedding anniversary.

BEN

Here's to us.

SYLVIA

Here's to us.

BEN

Forty-seven years.

SYLVIA

That's right.

BEN

That's a lot of years.

SYLVIA

Yes.

BEN

Gone by quickly.

SYLVIA

Yes, it has.

BEN

And slowly.

SYLVIA

That too.

BEN

Regrets?

SYLVIA

None that you don't know about.

BEN

Same here. What about that summer?

SYLVIA

You know how I feel about that.

BEN

I guess I do. (*Pause*) Do you think we should've had another kid?

SYLVIA

One was enough.

BEN

Yes. We had a good one.

SYLVIA

Yes.

BEN

No doubt about that. (*Extended pause*) But things would have been different, don't you think?

SYLVIA

Of course, things would have been different.

CHAPTER 1

BEN

Better?

SYLVIA

Maybe. Who knows? Why are you asking all these questions?

BEN

Just wondering.

SYLVIA

Every anniversary you do this.

BEN

I guess I do.

SYLVIA

Why?

BEN

I don't know. I guess anniversaries make me think, pause for a bit.

SYLVIA

Have you been unhappy?

BEN

Not really.

SYLVIA

Not really? What does that mean?

BEN

Nothing.

SYLVIA

No, go on. Say it.

BEN

I just think things would've been different if we had decided to have another kid.

SYLVIA

I couldn't.

BEN

I know.

SYLVIA

Ben was enough.

BEN

Ben the second. There won't be a Ben the third.

SYLVIA

No, there won't be.

BEN

Given the world today, that's probably a good thing.

SYLVIA

Can we talk about something else?

BEN

Sorry.

SYLVIA

You don't have to apologize. Just change the subject.

BEN

(*Pause*) I better get the grass cut tomorrow before the neighbors start to complain.

CHAPTER 1

                    SYLVIA

It needs it.

                     BEN

(*Picks up wine glass for another toast*) Here's to us.

                    SYLVIA

To another year.

                     BEN

A lot of years.

                    SYLVIA

Forty-seven and counting.

CHAPTER 2

CHILDHOOD AND ADOLESCENT DANGERS

STARBUCKS

I know when the two of you
get together, you can talk and talk.
I should have seen the signs:
You were complaining all morning
that you were tired of it all, fed up,
unhappy, ready for it to end.
I know things have been uncomfortable
for you, that they haven't been what you
expected, but neither have they been for me.
If it had been in the back seat of a cab
or even a bus, I'd understand, but
in Starbucks. You still have that smell.

I can picture the scene: Every Tuesday
for months now you'd meet. The two
of you leaning into each other, telling
secrets, hanging on each other's words.
I've seen the two of you carrying on.
Only this time, you, not wanting to leave
your latte, gulping it down, and then
doing it, right there. Were you so involved
that you forgot where you were? Didn't
you realize that Starbucks is not the place
for that? Did you say, "Excuse me, I have
to give birth now. I'll be back in a minute
and we can finish what we were saying"?
I know how you two are.

CHAPTER 2

And what will this do to our daughter
when she grows older? Will she be drawn
to conversations over coffee, confiding
to some future lover how his thick voice, echoing
from his cappuccino cup, turns her on, makes her
want to wake to the grind of fresh beans?

CHILDHOOD AND ADOLESCENT DANGERS

SUFFOCATING

I work two no good jobs
just to feed the four I got.
It's hard,
never knowing if there will be enough,
if I can keep the roof over our heads,
if I can take a sick one to the doctor.
It's hard,
after my mother died
and after my man left.
I don't have anybody
except my little ones.
So when another wanted in,
wanted to share in the little we have,
I had no choice.
Standing over him, I decided.
I could hardly breathe.
I stuffed his mouth and nose
with a picture of us five
my oldest had drawn
and taped them shut.
I let his little hands hold
my fingers until the breath
was gone and he let go.
It was hard,
but since I just had him last night,
he hadn't gotten my love
like my other babies have.
I wrapped him up in a plastic bag
hid him behind some towels
in the bathroom.
Thought everything would be fine
if I could just stop my bleeding,
but I bled and bled.
I guess I passed out

CHAPTER 2

and my babies called for help.
That's how the police knew.
That's why I'm here.
It's hard,
knowing they'll all be taken away.
I did it for the four of them.
Five would have been too hard.

BOOKCASE

CHARACTERS:

Peter, male, age 31, married to Cheryl
Cheryl, female, age 30, married to Peter

SETTING:

A small apartment.

AT RISE:

Peter and Cheryl, standing over a fallen bookcase, books everywhere.

CHERYL

You need to clean this mess up.

PETER

I will. (*Stands bookcase upright and starts to place books on the shelves.*)

CHERYL

You're not going to put those books back on those shelves, are you?

PETER

Where else would I put them?

CHERYL

Anywhere else. But not there. Just get rid of them.

PETER

I can't get rid of my books. I need them for my work.

CHERYL

Maybe when you were in graduate school, you should have taken a class in how to place books on a bookcase. English majors should learn something useful.

CHAPTER 2

> PETER

Very funny.

> CHERYL

I wasn't trying to be funny.

> PETER

Look, after I put it together, I secured it to the wall. Remember, you said you thought it was fine.

> CHERYL

But I didn't know you were going to load so many damn books on it. Your books were nearly piled to the ceiling. I told you you had too many up there.

> PETER

It felt safe to me.

> CHERYL

But it wasn't, was it?

> PETER

No, I guess it wasn't, but it would have been fine if you had been watching him.

> CHERYL

Don't try and put that on me.

> PETER

He was in here alone. Right?

> CHERYL

I was cooking dinner and I thought he was playing with his toys.

> PETER

Well, he wasn't, was he?

CHERYL

I kept checking on him.

PETER

Well, I guess you didn't check enough.

CHERYL

And I guess you didn't secure the bookcase, did you?

(*Cheryl begins to cry. Peter continues picking up books and putting them on the book shelves. After putting several away, he finds a child's book and freezes, staring at it.*)

PETER

Do you think this is what he was after?

CHERYL

I don't think he was after any of your books.

PETER

No, this is his book. Look. *Fox in Socks*. Remember, last night after you were reading to him, you took him to bed and I was straightening up in here. I put the book on this shelf. I bet he was climbing up the shelves to get it when it went over.

CHERYL

That would explain what he was doing, how it happened.

PETER

Yeah. That explains it. (*Looks down at the book in his hand.*) What do you want me to do with this?

CHERYL

I don't know. Throw it away.

PETER

(*Walks over to the trash and drops the book in.*) Done.

CHAPTER 2

                        CHERYL

Good.

                        PETER

That's what we have to do with all our "you did this," and "you did that." We need to drop such talk in the trash.

                        CHERYL

I am not sure if I can. You can't blame yourself when you lose a child that way. It's just too much.

                        PETER

No one is to blame. It was an accident. (*Begins to approach Cheryl, but stops himself.*)

                        CHERYL

I want to believe that.

                        PETER

Me too.

CURIOSITY

I wonder if I can:
    grab my cat's tail
    eat my fingers
    get out of my mommy's arms
    ride on my dog
    throw this full cup of milk up in the air
    crawl over to that fireplace
    shove this peanut up my nose
    move this chair so I can get another cookie
    share my cookie with my dog
    paint with what I have in my diaper all over that wall
    give Teddy a bath in the toilet
    chew on my toes
    slide out of my highchair
    drop this spaghetti on top my head
    bite my daddy's arm
    jump up and down in this slippery tub
    put this little paper clip in my mouth
    guide this crayon into my ear
    climb on that bottom shelve in the refrigerator to reach my juice
    roll over while mommy is changing my diaper
    stand on the back of this sofa
    pull those pretty ornaments off our Christmas tree
    lick the bottom of my daddy's shoe
    use a glass like mommy's to drink
    open that door and go outside
    taste that dead bug
    take off my clothes and wash myself in the sink
    cook dinner for mommy and daddy
    wake daddy up by hitting him with his phone
    change the channel on TV by pushing all these buttons
    show mommy and daddy what my cat put in the litter
    yank on mommy's hair
    make my arm go down this heating vent

CHAPTER 2

      cut my hair
      run holding these scissors
      take those pills that mommy and daddy take
      dine on some of this mud
      do whatever I want

TODDLER FOUND IN SCHOOLYARD

It could be that moment when she is coloring her numbers,
tracking their proper order as they snake around the page.
Maybe when facing her elementary writing tablet
she'll hesitate just a slight second before dotting her "i."
Or, perhaps, when the bell rings and her friends rush
to recess, she will linger, her hard shoes stuck, unable
to run to Double Dutch. She will hang by the door frame,
look out, and see herself, one-and-a-half-years old, dressed
in nothing more than a diaper and shirt, sitting up
in a snow bank, near the dumpster in the schoolyard,
her blood seeping from her stab wounds, a steak knife
still in her back, and her mother walking away.
Then, she'll understand how the numbers add up, the abc's
of it all, and the cruel grind of the classroom clock.

CHAPTER 2

BOY

1.

Been sitting on this corner for twelve years, watching that old building fall down. Seen more than I can tell. Seen all kinds go in and out of that place. Some for their quick love. Some just for a night's sleep. Some for their steady fix. When the children went in, I knew they were up to no good. I said to my old friend Matthew, "Look at them children." But Lord, I never imagined that death was waiting for that little child.

2.

Sure as shit they dropped him, right out of that window. Landed on his side, leaving one half fine, but the other—splattered. Scrambled eggs. Hard to believe what those people do to each other. Scrape him up and tag him so we can get out of here.

3.

Lord, deliver us out of this damn place.
Let us take our precious babies and run;
This place ain't fit for anyone.

4.

We all went to lunch today—had that Super Caesar's at Mary's—and John starts telling about that five-year-old boy who was dropped out of a fourteen story window by two other kids, one ten and the other eleven. His brother fought to stop them but couldn't. They killed that poor child cause he wouldn't steal for them. After I got home, I read that story over and over. Did you see it? When John told us about it, my tears came up. I couldn't stop crying and everyone was looking away like I'm crazy. No one would face it. We just went back to the office. We couldn't even live off his death.

CHILDHOOD AND ADOLESCENT DANGERS

5.

Momma, I should've done more. I swear to God I tried. I tried to stop them. I tried to grab him, Momma, but he ain't here no more.

Momma, they were stronger than me, but I'm going to grow strong too. Then they'll see what they can do. Momma, I know what they done to you.

Momma, I was holding his hand, had my hand over his when he went out. Then it pulled away when he went down. I was holding his hand, Momma.

6.

When I heard I wouldn't believe, couldn't believe that had happened to my baby. My little baby, sweet as anybody's business, never did nothing wrong. That child could pull love from a turnip. They dropped my baby out of that window for change. Oh, my sweet baby!

And now my other baby cries, swearing revenge, saying he's going to be strong. Oh Lord, don't make him mean. Don't put that poison in his head.

CHAPTER 2

LONG RANGE

He calls himself
Dougie the cowboy,
gallops through their house
on his five-year-old legs.

When I phone, he cries.
"Be a big cowboy,
stop crying.
Daddy will see you soon."

"When is soon?" he asks.
"Maybe in a few weeks, buddy."
"That's not soon.
Come tonight."

"I can't but it won't be long
before I get to see my boy.
Let me talk to your mother."

Bang Bang
You're Dead

"He waits by the phone every week."
"I know.
When can I see him?"
"Soon."

CHILDHOOD AND ADOLESCENT DANGERS

CHILDHOOD DISTRESS

1.

After my mother walked me the four blocks to the day camp I would be attending and back home again, I told her I knew how to get there and back. On the first day, I marched my seven-year-old body straight to the camp, but when it was time to return home, I took a right instead of the left that would have taken me back to familiar territory. I was carrying under my left arm a wet bathing suit rolled in a towel much larger than I needed to dry off, and in my right hand a lunch bag, empty, except for the two Oreo cookies I was saving for when I got home. I walked and walked and began to realize that nothing looked familiar. I walked some more hoping I'd soon recognize my surroundings. I finally figured I had taken a wrong turn so I turned again and walked some more. My legs were getting tired. I turned again. I walked some more. Then it struck me: I was lost. I would never find my way home. I plopped down on the hot sidewalk. Tears rushed down my face. I reached in my lunch bag and pulled out one my Oreos. Tears and snot mixed with the Oreo taste. A kind woman who saw me saved the day, but I hold the image of me sitting on the burning hot concrete, tears and snot streaming down, eating my last meal.

2.

When I hurt my little finger playing junior high football and the doctor said that my season was over, I was elated. I hated that I was expected to play because I was a guy. I never liked being hit or hitting anyone else. I never stopped thinking, "Hey, I can get hurt out here." Once, during practice, Jake, who was the biggest and faster player on our team, was running full speed toward the goal. I had a chance to make a tackle, but I stopped running. I decided trying to tackle him would be a foolish thing for me to do. I never liked playing the game. It always felt like I was never man enough.

3.

My brother, Gus, and I shared ownership of a Daisy BB gun that my dad gave us despite my mother's objections. The Daisy gun was just

CHAPTER 2

powerful enough to knock a can off a fence if you hit it at the right angle. BBs shot from our Daisy moved, not in a straight line toward the target, but more in a rainbow arch. You had to take that into account when shooting. Bobby, the kid who lived directly across the street from us, had a pump BB gun. I don't remember the kind, but I know it wasn't named after a flower, and if you pumped it enough, it would shoot through a piece of wood. With Bobby's gun, we shot coconuts down from the fifty-foot palm tree in his yard. One day, Gus, who was five years older than I, and Bobby, who was three years older, decided we should have a battle. "Since you're only seven and it's hard for you to pump Bobby's gun, you get the Daisy," Gus said. "We'll have to share Bobby's pump gun." That sounded like a good deal to me. I seldom got the Daisy all to myself. They told me that they would count to one hundred and then they were coming for me. They were sure I would just run home, but I hid right under the porch, ready to get them when they came out the door. When I heard the door open, I stood up and fired. I missed. I turned and started to run, but when I looked back, a BB found my upper lip. "You shot me," I cried, realizing for the first time the possible consequences of our game. Gus came running toward me. "Don't tell mom! Don't tell mom!" he pleaded, over and over. I headed for home, wanting mom to fix my wound and trying to figure out how words might win the war.

4.

I was chasing dragonflies in our backyard when it happened. It was a hot summer day and I was barefoot. As I leaped to catch a blue one, I came down on a glass jar. It shattered under my weight. I looked down and saw my blood on a broken piece of glass. I stared for the longest time, amazed at what I was seeing. I turned my foot to see if that was where the blood came from. I was cut underneath my little toe. I decided I needed mom's help and started walking up the stairs. On each step, drops of blood were left behind. When I reached the top, the tears began. "Mom, I cut myself," I cried out. She was taking a bath, but called me into to bathroom, even though I was beyond the age of being in the room when mom was bathing. "Where are you

CHILDHOOD AND ADOLESCENT DANGERS

cut?" she asked, covering herself with the shower curtain. "My toe," I said. "Well, put your foot in here." I did as I was told. The tub water turned red. We were on our way to the emergency room before I knew it. Five stitches later, I was on my way back home. Neither the cut nor the stitches hurt. My tears were tears of fear that could only see red.

5.

What I remember is that I was playing with my toy soldiers and I started feeling like I had pins and needles sticking me all over my body. I told my mom and she felt my forehead. Immediately, I felt her alarm. "Let's get you to bed." She put a cool washcloth on my forehead as she took my temperature. After reading the thermometer, she called the doctor. Her voice sounded urgent, but she spoke too softly for me to make out the words. She hung up and reported that the doctor would be coming to the house. This was back when doctors still did such things. My mother sat on the side of my bed, holding my hand and rubbing my arm. I have some sense that I kept falling into unconsciousness. Maybe, it was just falling asleep. I would wake and mom would be there, still rubbing my arm. When the doctor arrived, I was examined and given a shot. Outside my room, I heard my mother ask, "Are you sure it's not polio?" "I'm sure," he answered.

6.

I awoke on my tenth birthday excited, anticipating the birthday surprises that might come my way. As I came into the kitchen, mom gave me her usual morning greeting. No mention of my birthday. I hung around the house for a while waiting for some birthday acknowledgment. Nothing. Dad went off to work. My brother and sister went about their daily routines. I decided to go outside and play. At lunch time, I came in for a peanut butter and jelly sandwich, but again, no one said anything about my special day. By four o'clock that afternoon, I couldn't stop myself from asking my mom if she remembered that it was my birthday. "Oh my," she said. She seemed preoccupied with something, but truly sorry she had forgotten my birthday. She went straight to her purse. "Here's seven dollars," she said, giving me all

CHAPTER 2

the money she had in her wallet. "Go buy yourself something at the toy store." I took the money and walked the few blocks to the store. I picked out a football helmet. It was blue with a padded chin strap. The only time I ever wore it was at the store. I never knew why mom was so preoccupied.

7.

I went to a small high school that had limited sports facilities. There was no gym on school grounds for our basketball team. When we had practice or played another team for a home game, we used a public recreational center about two miles from our school. Our coach pushed us and we weren't bad—got to the state play-offs one year. It was the same year several players were injured in a car wreck. I saw the wreck coming. It was dark and raining by the time we got out of practice. Larry agreed to give six of us a ride home, and we started down the long, two-lane, winding road that led to and from the gym. I was sitting in the radio seat, and sensing that Larry was driving too fast, I braced myself against the dash. The road was lined with large oak trees. Large oaks, wet pavement, and too much speed are not a good combination. We hit one of the oaks head on. My teammates' sounds were unlike anything I'd ever heard before. Cries. Curses. Calls for help. Some were just moaning. A few of us were able to get out of the car. I realized I was the only one who wasn't hurt. I yelled, "Help! Help!" but we were too far away from the houses I spotted down the road for anyone to hear. I ran toward the lights, ran with a desperation I'd never felt before. I kept yelling for help. A good-hearted woman met me on the street, and after I told her what happened, she called the police. Two ambulances arrived and we were all taken to the hospital. A broken leg, a shattered wrist, many cuts and bruises, and some sprains and soreness. Enough to lose three players from our team that year. I was the last to receive a doctor's attention. "I'm fine," I said, "What about my friends?" "They'll all be fine," the doctor replied. Even after the doctor's assuring words, I kept thinking, "There was a lot of blood." I tried to take a breath, a deep long breath, but my breath was shallow.

DON'T

Don't come near the hot stove.
Don't put that in the electrical socket.
Don't play with matches.
Don't eat that.
Don't get out of your bed.
Don't climb on the furniture.
Don't run with a scissors.
Don't go in the street.
Don't speak to strangers.
Don't stuff so much in your mouth.
Don't tell anyone about our little secret.
Don't fight with your brother.
Don't leave your shit all over the place.
Don't use that language in this house.
Don't you dare bring home those kind of grades again.
Don't bother your mother.
Don't tell me "no."
Don't annoy your father when he's been drinking.
Don't turn on that noise in here.
Don't talk back.
Don't get on my nerves.
Don't tell anyone how you got that bruise.
Don't stay out too late.
Don't even look at your mom's pills or my booze.
Don't hang out with those kids.
Don't touch yourself.
Don't fool with my gun.
Don't be fooling around with those boys.
Don't tell me not to put my hand there.
Don't act so angry.
Don't forget everything we did for you.
Don't disobey your father.
Don't leave this house without my permission.
Don't tell me about that.
Don't let your childhood haunt you.

CHAPTER 2

DEAD MAN'S ALLEY

Behind my childhood home was an old garbage alley that was no longer in use. The city allowed it to grow over. Tall fences, no longer with entries, lined each side. Only a thin, curving path littered with bottle caps, broken glass, and various discarded household items cut its way from one side of the block to the other side. Small clearings could be found within the foliage, places where kids, like my brother, Gus, and I could imagine we were hiding from the Indians before we would go running out, cap guns in hand. We were told it was too dangerous to play there which made it all the more seductive and frightening. Gus and I would usually enter on the side by the dry cleaners, a short walk around the corner from our house.

"Look," Gus said, pointing to the ground. I glanced down but didn't see anything out of the ordinary. Gus fell to his knees and started digging with a stick he grabbed. He was carving around something, but I still couldn't make it out. "Look," he repeated, "It's a skull. Help me dig it up." I kneeled beside him and began pulling the dirt away as he loosened it with his stick. More and more was exposed, and Gus was soon able to lift it from its burial place. He stood holding it in his hands and then dropped it to the ground. "It's human. It's a human skull," he said, backing away.

We were still staring at the skull when we heard a man call out, "Oh my God! Get out of here! Get!" At first, Gus and I thought he was talking to us, but when we looked down the alley, we could see that he wasn't paying any attention to us. He had a broom in his hand and was jabbing at something. We could see people gathering. "Be careful. Don't let him get you," someone said. Gus kicked the skull until it was under a small bush. I watched it roll, its toothless mouth wide open, its eyes meeting mine with each turn. "We'll come back later," Gus said. "Let's go see what's going on." We ran down the alley. The crowd had grown larger and formed a circle in the middle of the street. I maneuvered myself between two adults and felt one of them put a hand on my shoulder, holding me back. "An alligator," I said to myself. Its head was raised, its mouth slightly open, and its tail curled around. It must have been seven or eight feet long.

CHILDHOOD AND ADOLESCENT DANGERS

"If you saw this out in the swamp, no one would bat an eye. But here in the middle of New Orleans, I can hardly believe it," a man said.

"Someone should call animal control," a woman in tattered slippers suggested, but she didn't move from the circle.

"I bet it escaped from Audubon Park Zoo. That's only about four blocks from here," said someone else.

The man who had chased it with his broom into the street offered another explanation: "I think it was someone's pet. You know, one of those baby gators you can buy. I bet it got away and found its home in the back room of my cleaners. That's where I found it." People seemed to be dismissing that hypothesis, but then he added, "You see, I never go back there, because that room always has water sitting in it from all the washers. I just thought I'd check it this morning because we've been running those washers hard. When I opened the door, there it was, staring at me. I bet it's been feeding on the rats." People were nodding when I blurted out, "I bet he ate that man we found in the alley." All eyes moved from the alligator to me. My brother looked like I betrayed him, told everyone something I shouldn't have. "You found a man in the alley?" someone asked.

"Just his skull," I answered and then added, "I guess it was a man's." Just then two men from animal control arrived and focus shifted back to the alligator. They quickly put a noose around the alligator's mouth. They were trying to guide the gator into a crate when the police pulled their car on the sidewalk next to the crowd. They got out and instructed everyone, like we didn't know what we were doing, to back up. After a bit, the animal control men managed to get the gator in the crate, slid it up a ramp into their truck, and slowly pulled away. The circle broke apart. People were moving on, shaking their heads, when I saw the woman in tattered slippers talking to the police and pointing at me. One of the officers walked over to me: "I understand you found a body in the alley that you think the alligator ate?" he questioned. Gus answered for me: "We just found a skull. That's all."

"Can you show it to me?"

"Sure, it's just a little ways down the alley." The first officer waved to the second officer to join us, and we headed toward the skull.

CHAPTER 2

Several people, including the slippers woman, started to follow, but they were told to stay where they were.

"It's under that bush," Gus said, pointing.

"Is that where you found it?" one of the officers asked.

"No. We found it right over here," I said, moving toward the hole we dug. The officer dug around the hole with his foot. "Nothing here," he called to the other officer. The other officer was holding the skull, his thumb hooked into one of the eye sockets. "We'll just take this with us," he said, lifting it to waist level. "You boys be careful playing in this alley," the other one added. Gus and I stood there, watching them walk back to their car, the skull swinging between them. On the way, they stopped and said something to people waiting at the end of the alley. People chuckled.

"What are they laughing at?" I asked Gus.

"I don't know, but I'm sure they're taking that skull somewhere to examine it."

"You think so?" I said. I trusted my older brother to know such things.

"Yeah. They didn't make a big deal about it because they didn't want to make us worry," he explained. "That alligator ate everything but the skull."

"Why didn't it eat the skull?"

"Too hard, I guess."

"We ought to get out of here," I said, beginning to feel frightened. "That gator could have eaten us."

"It got whoever that skull belonged to," he said in a way that scared me even more. "From now on," he continued, "we're going to call this alley, Dead Man's Alley."

I nodded. Then I said, "I want to go home."

BOBBY

As a climber of trees
he was the best, going
higher than my imagination
would permit. He moved
without thought, always
connected, a foot, a hand
a foot, on and on, over
and over, up, to the top.
Far below, I would calculate
each step before going on
and then stop, wedged
between safe branches,
content to watch, until
his mother's chilling call,
"Get down from there!"
brought him down too soon.
They rushed his broken bones
away as he cried,
"Did you see how high
I was? Did you see?"
When he healed, he was sent
to an all boys school that
makes men of boyhood friends,
then business college. Now,
having put down his roots
and branching out, Robert hangs
from the financial pages. Dollars
fall around him like autumn leaves.

CHAPTER 2

BACK YARD

Underneath the concrete figure-eight patio where the two circles of eight joined, directly to the side of the sliding glass door, beside the bird of paradise plant that we wrapped in white sheets whenever the weather threatened, my parents planned to build the bomb shelter.

We drove from lot to lot, pricing, picking just the right one for our family of four and our house dog, Happy, who was permanently put into the yard after the new carpets were laid. We were fenced in mostly by our neighbors' design—blond brick running the full length of the back property line, lattice on one side, slats on the other. Our own link completed the closure.

Happy died the same day I was going long for my brother's pass and my leg met the hard edge of our brick house and needed stitching. "He died of neglect," I accused, refusing to accept any responsibility. For weeks I found his fur as I edged the figure-eight. When the workers dug down for the shelter, I swear I saw broken bones in a bottomless grave.

SCHOOL INSTRUCTION

1. SPANISH CLASS

I should say from the beginning that I was not a very good student in Spanish. Perhaps it was because I didn't start my Spanish education until the tenth grade or, more likely, because I found my Spanish teacher, Mrs. Aimes, my least favorite teacher. Mrs. Aimes was a thin woman who stood straight as a two-by-four. She pulled her silver and black hair in a tight bun on a forty-five degree angle from the top of her head which made her long neck seem even longer. She was from Spain and mostly spoke Spanish in class. That meant I mostly didn't understand a word she said. I never had the desire or discipline to memorize the Spanish words for the things I could more easily name in English. Mrs. Aimes was not one to let my indifference, or should I say laziness, pass. She taught by the force of her presence.

One day Mrs. Aimes was passing back our mid-term Spanish tests. As she went around the room, she would address each test taker with a brief remark: "Bueno, Pam." "You can do better, Mike." "Better than your last quiz, Natalie." I was sitting in my desk dreading my turn for Mrs. Aimes's public commentary about my performance on the exam. I knew I hadn't done well. She came up behind me. "Ronald," she began. She was the only teacher I ever had that called me Ronald. I much preferred Ronnie or Ron. "Please stand up." I got out of my desk and stood facing the front of the class. She remained behind me, holding my test. "Class," she continued, "take a good look at Ronald. This is what a thirty-seven looks like." I felt myself turning red. I wanted more than anything to sit back down. "There is a big difference," she went on, speaking in plain English to make sure everyone got her point, "between a student and a pupil. A student is someone who studies and will make something of him or herself. A pupil is someone who just takes up space. Ronald, you are a pupil."

What happened next still surprises me as I recount this tale. It came from a place that I still don't think of as part of me. Out of my embarrassment and anger, I reached for the English words that I thought would be of equal power to hers. I turned, stared right her, and said, "And you're a bitch."

CHAPTER 2

The class froze. Mrs. Aimes moved to the front of the room. After a moment, she continued her lesson on the difference between students and pupils. "And pupils get sent to the principal's office." She was pointing at the door. I gathered my book bag and started walking toward the door. I said "bitch" one more time just loud enough for everyone to hear.

"Go," Mrs. Aimes said. I left.

I had to explain to Mr. Montgonery my version of why I was sent to his office. After telling my side of things, he told me to go to my next class when the next bell rang and that I would be hearing from him. Waiting to learn the consequences of my action settled around me as if I had fifty pound weights in every one of my pockets. The next day Mr. Montgonery informed me that my parents had to come to school. I knew that meant I'd be grounded for an extended period of time. I also got detention for a week, and I had to apologize to Mrs. Aimes. I apologized, but I didn't mean it.

Back in the tenth grade, I would have never guessed I would have become a teacher. Occasionally, I think of Mrs. Aimes's distinction between students and pupils, and I must admit that I have seen some classroom behaviors in keeping with Mrs. Aimes's definition of a pupil. I've never, however, shared that perception with a student. That's one thing I'd say I learned from Mrs. Aimes.

2. THE TRIPLETS

They looked as if they had just stepped out of one of those teen fashion magazines—long hair with sweeping curls at the bottom, make-up applied with just the right red touches, stylish clothes from head to foot. Meggie Johnson, Ali Brooks, and Jenny Swanson are their names, but, behind their backs, everyone called them The Triplets. The Triplets were always together, giggling, whispering, pointing. They usually walked in a straight line and seemed annoyed if they had to break rank to get through a doorway. You never knew who would be in the center as they marched on. They moved with the confidence of a seasoned knife thrower. Few were a part of their inner circle; fewer still were considered worthy of their company. Outsiders saw them as some form of deluxe vacuum that would suck up those they considered debris and quickly disposed of them. They were not well liked, but they were always noticed, and for some who had become their targets, they were feared. Chuck, a frequent target, would begin to shake when he saw them.

Chuck wasn't my best friend, but I knew him pretty well, and every now and then we played video games together. Chuck was a big guy, fat really, about 300 pounds I guess. He usually kept to himself at school, but he could be a lot of fun when it was just the two of us together. "I wish The Triplets didn't call me Chuck the Chub," he confessed one day. "I know I'm big. They don't have to announce it every time they see me."

"Don't pay any attention to them," I said.

"That's easy for you to say. They don't call you names."

"You're right, but I've seen how they can be. One day they were standing by the outside water fountain, and as I was walking by, I just said, 'Hi.' I think it was Ali who spoke first: 'Were we talking to you?' she says. 'Did we invite you over here?' Jenny says, and then, before I could say a word, Meggie says, 'Bye.' I wasn't even planning to stop. I was on my way to class. They're just mean that way," I said.

"I don't want them calling me Chuck the Chub. That's all."

Just a couple of days later Chuck and I were hanging out by my locker and the Triplets came strutting by. "There's Chuck the Chub," one of them said. The other two laughed a little and they were gone down the hall. Chuck just looked down and shook his head. "Bitches," he muttered under his breath.

Now here is the place in the story where I wish I could tell you that I stood up for Chuck and The Triplets never said that to Chuck again. I wish I could tell you that they got what they deserved. You know, like in the movies, when the kids who think they're so cool get it in the end. I wish I could tell you that I ran after The Triplets after they said that to Chuck, and I said just the right thing to them, and Chuck laughed, and everybody in school heard about it, and things were never the same for them again. But, what really happened, I said, "Forget about it, Chuck. Fuck'em." Nothing changed. They were like that all through high school, and Chuck and I were like we were,

CHAPTER 2

always trying to think of something to say or do that would stop them. They never stopped thinking they were better than everybody else. I wonder, now that we've all graduated, if they ever realized how cruel they were, if they ever had any regrets. I wonder if they know how they were.

3. CHICKEN SHIT

He showed up at my high school wanting to know where I was, but I had already left for home. He said to one of my friends, "Tell Ron I'm looking for him." Before then, I knew. Liz told me earlier that day that her boyfriend was coming for me because I asked her for a date. A small smile appeared on her face as she shared this information. "Really," I said, "for asking you out?" Prior to that moment, I did not know she had a boyfriend. When I asked her if she wanted to hang out sometime, she shrugged, "No thanks" as if I was the tenth person she had to say no to that day. I thought that was the end of it.

"You can't try to make a move on someone when they're already hooked up," she replied.

"All I did was ask you out," I said, still expressing my disbelief.

"That doesn't matter," she said and walked away.

Liz moved through the world in a way one might associate with a older woman. She seemed experienced, aware of what most of my friends and I were still discovering. She wore more make-up than most of the girls I knew, and when she walked, her hips had a definite sway. The top of her breasts inched above her low cut blouses. She had a way of looking at you that seemed inviting. My mistake was to have noticed, to think the invitation was sent directly to me. I soon realized that I was just someone she used to make her boyfriend jealous.

The next day when I was outside washing my mom's car he found me. He drove up with two of his friends in one of those souped-up cars that sounded as if it was always ready to start a race. All three of them jumped out, formed a perfect triangle, and came straight at me. "I'm Brad. Liz is my girlfriend," the guy at the head of the triangle stated, underlining the "my."

"Look," I said, "I don't want any trouble."

"And I don't want any excuses, you fuck-face," he said as he threw his first punch. He was holding a small lead pipe in each of his fists. With the first blow, I was down. He jumped on me and hit me several more times. I did not fight back; I just put my arms around my head to protect myself. He got up, stood over me, and yelled, "You leave Liz alone. You hear me, you fuck-head. Or I'll be back." Then, he and his friends were gone, leaving the scene with tires screeching. I lifted myself from the ground and made my way to the car's side mirror: a fat, bloody lip, a slight cut above my left eye, and three red welts on the right side of my face. I slowly gathered the supplies I was using to wash the car, even though I hadn't finished the job. I put everything away and went inside.

"What happened to you?" my mother wanted to know. I tried to explain, but I couldn't quite make sense of it. My mother, working on my wounds, decided she should call the police. "No, mom, please don't," I said, believing that would only make things worse. After arguing back and forth, she finally gave in to my wishes. "If that boy ever comes around here again or hits you again, you tell me and we'll put a stop to this," was her final remark.

The next day in school I saw Liz. "I met your boyfriend, Brad, yesterday. What an asshole!" I said.

"He told me you acted like a chicken shit little girl. He would have fucked you up more, but you didn't even fight back. He said you were pathetic." She turned and left as fast as Brad had the day before. Her summary account of yesterday's event, though, stayed with me, ate at me. I tried to make sense of it all: Did I act like a coward? I thought shortly after it was all over that I should've fought back, but it all happened so quickly. Maybe I was stunned by his first punch. Maybe I knew I couldn't fight all three of them. Did that make me a coward? What's a coward anyway? I didn't run. I didn't let my mom call the police. I didn't cry out, "please stop" or anything. I didn't even know this guy. Why would I want to fight him? I didn't do anything wrong with Liz. I just asked her out. That's all. Why would he want to hit me? What did Liz tell him I did? These thoughts ran around my head for days.

CHAPTER 2

A couple months after the fight, I stumbled into Brad and Liz at a football game. I was startled, froze for a moment. "Don't worry, you little chicken shit. I'm not going to hit you again," Brad said and they both laughed. I just looked at them and then it struck me. I've been defined, named chicken shit. For them, and probably for others who heard their side of things, that's who I am. Chicken shit. Named justly or not, I am now seen that way. Chicken shit.

Looking back, even after all these years, their defining assessment still has some anchoring power for me. I am a chicken shit. That's how culture works. Even when you know better, you feel its pressures. Some days, I feel proud of that label.

MANACLE MOM

I was a wild one.
No one could tell me
nothing.
I knew it all,
didn't listen to
nobody.
Found trouble alright,
without even hardly
looking.
My girls
were at that age,
filled, like I was,
with the poison.
It starts in the mind
saying you got the answers.
Then it moves in your body,
slow at first, but
once it takes hold,
those urges keep coming.
You can't control them.
You want to be free
from those thoughts,
but you'll want them boys.
That's the worst
cause you'll make a fool of yourself.
You'll want them to hold you,
but they only want one thing,
and you'll want it too,
but if you give it,
they're gone,
and you're stuck with a baby
you got no right wanting.
I didn't want that for my girls.
So when they started not listening,

CHAPTER 2

I chained them together to their bed.
They started acting up
so I hit them a few times only
to show them I meant business.
They learned quick I was serious.
They were shaking and crying.
I told them that
I'd rather them shake here
than under some boy,
and I'd rather them cry
because of me
than because of some boy.
A mother has to take care
of her girls.
She has to teach
them right.
A mother mothers
from the womb.

FIFTEEN HIGH SCHOOL MICRO-DRAMAS

1.

Sam: Okay, let's finish picking sides.
Ron: Pick me.
Sam: I'm not going to pick you. You're no good. I pick Mike.

2.

Ron: You can do better than her.
Mike: What's wrong with her? I like her.
Ron: I don't know. She just doesn't seem good enough for you.

3.

Jim: Who wants to go get some pizza?
Ron: I do.
Jim: I didn't mean you.

4.

Ron: You are such a bitch.
Jen: I wish you wouldn't call me that.
Ron: Then stop acting like a bitch.

5.

Coach: Do you have a brain? If so, get it out of your ass and remember the play. You go behind, not in front of that man.
Ron: Sorry coach.
Coach: Don't be sorry. Get it right, dumb ass, or you can sit on the bench.

6.

Ron: No matter what we hand in, we get the same grade. I think we should call Mrs. Trocher, Mrs. Atrocious.
Bobby: Yeah. That's good.
Ron: I'm going to tell everyone that's her new name.

CHAPTER 2

7.

Faye: Who taught you how to dance? You look like a convulsing chicken.
Ron: I was just moving to the beat.
Faye: Well don't, unless you want to look ridiculous.

8.

Ron: You put your dick in her vagina, not her clitoris, you idiot.
Danny: I thought it was the clitoris.
Ron: I know you did. You idiot.

9.

Teacher: You don't know the difference between "there" and "their" yet? Where have you been?
Ron: I've been here.
Teacher: I'm not seeing any evidence of that.

10.

Ron: You want me to spit this beer on you?
Camille: You wouldn't dare.
Ron: Want to bet?

11.

Lizzie: Now, who are you and what are you doing here?
Ron: I'm Ron. Remember, I met you just last week and you said I should come over for the pool party today.
Lizzie: I don't remember that.

12.

Ron: Why won't you put your hand there?
Susan: Because I don't want to.
Ron: You're such a tease.

CHILDHOOD AND ADOLESCENT DANGERS

13.

Carol: Where did you get that shirt? It looks like it came from your dad's closet.
Ron: I just got it.
Carol: Well, I wouldn't wear it again if I were you.

14.

Ron: I can't believe you think that's funny.
Deb: It is funny.
Ron: It's not, so stop telling everybody that stupid joke.

15.

Margo: You think you're such hot shit. But let me tell you, you're not. You're nothing. Nothing at all.
Ron: I must be something.
Margo: No, you're not even nothing.

CHAPTER 2

STUCK

When I don't have to talk to Mr. Hamm, particularly when he's been drinking, I'm happy. He looked strange in the trash can, just his bottom half sticking out, his hands squeezed into his side. Maybe he lost something, I thought, or threw out a drop of booze he wanted back. I didn't know.

I said hello, trying not to laugh. He mumbled some reply I couldn't make out. I just assumed he was drunk again, and I wasn't going to get paid. I told him I was going to put his paper by the door and I left. Next day he was in there too. He must have heard me coming or the paper hit against his door. He wiggled his fat fingers at me. By the third day I knew something was wrong. Said "hi" once, normal, and then again, loud. Nothing.

They had to cut him out. He had been drunk. He had stumbled off the porch, bottle in hand, backwards into the barrel. His head, at the bottom, was sliced open, blood mixed with spilled bourbon. The maggots began to feed.

Each day I do my route, I pass that rusting metal, wondering what life it still might breed.

CHILDHOOD AND ADOLESCENT DANGERS

DRINKING

When I was growing up, the legal drinking age in New Orleans was eighteen. That meant kids started drinking around fifteen. I was no exception. My brother, Gus, gave me one of his old IDs and I was set. My friends and I learned quickly which bars would let you in without checking your ID, which bars would let you in if you just had something you could show them, and which bars made entry tough for the underage drinker. The Attic fit the first category and my friends and I trusted that we would likely find someone we knew there if we showed up. Located on the second floor, the ceiling of The Attic was slanted, about five feet tall at its lowest point and about seven feet tall at its height. We thought that was cool. I often drank more than I should there before finding my way home. By some miracle, I always made it home without a mishap. This is a tale about such high school acts of stupidity.

I could tell you about how my friend, Larry, and I would often stop on our way to basketball practice and have a couple of beers. I'm sure we would have played better ball if we hadn't stopped, but I don't think our coach ever knew. I could describe how on a dare I spit, after drinking too much, some beer in my date's face, and how she was still willing to go out with me. I could admit that the night after I won the Louisiana State Junior Golf Championship, I put a sheet over my head after too many celebratory drinks and ran up and down the hall of a dorm at a local college, yelling, "I'm a ghost. I'm a ghost." When other junior golfers came out of their dorm rooms, my friend, George, said, "This is your state champion." I drove home the next day, trophy in hand, to my proud parents. But the tale I should tell is the one I remember least well.

Jackie and I had been dating a long time by high school standards, maybe three months. We both loved Peter, Paul, and Mary and decided that we would save our money so we could get tickets when they came to town. We managed to get two seats, close to the stage. The day of the concert, one of my friends called around 1:00 and said his parents had gone out of town and he was having a pool party. I went right over and started drinking. I don't know how much I drank, but the next thing I can recall was sitting next to Jackie listening to Peter, Paul and Mary. I learned from my friends that I had passed out, that they threw me in a cold shower, dressed me for my date, and dropped Jackie and me off at the concert. I also learned that Jackie didn't want to go out with me anymore. I don't remember the evening, except for that momentary realization that I was at the concert. I don't remember anything I said to Jackie that night. I don't remember getting home. I don't remember those lost hours. I do remember laughing about it with my friends the next day.

IN SEARCH OF A DRINKING SONG

She drank and drank and drank some more.
She laughed and laughed and fell against the door.
She partied so hard; she partied so long,
drinking shots and beers to the cheers of the throng.
They lost count at twelve or twenty-four.
It all seemed fun until she fell to the floor.
Too busy chugging what their friends had dared,
no one noticed and no one cared.
Then her old lover, drunk, sank to her side.
"I'm sorry," he slurred, "Give me one more chance."
He saw his hopes die in her eyes so wide.
The medics slid her into the ambulance.
Fitting end for the end of October
and now they drink alone, dead, cold sober.

CHAPTER 3

JESUS CHRONICLES

FOR THE CHILDREN

A man in dirty jeans and a sweatshirt is holding three prizes from the mechanical-arm machine—a rabbit with bent whiskers, a white bear with a red ribbon around its neck, and a penguin wearing a tux and top hat. A woman is working on the fourth.

"Look at how many things you two have won," I say, noticing them right after I add my name to the waiting list for a table at Steak 'n Shake.

"My mom is the one who plays," the man of forty-something says.

"I'm playing for the children," she reports without taking her eye off the movement of the arm. "One night Jesus came to me and he told me I had a gift. 'Go play for the children,' he said," she adds as she lifts and drops a baby doll with straight golden hair made of yarn into the hole. The hair on the baby doll's head looks just like hers.

"She's been playing ever since Jesus spoke to her," her son says, happy to confirm her account. "She's won hundreds of prizes."

"Jesus watches over me. He guides my hand. Some days he says, 'Okay, you got enough now. You done enough good.' Jesus is telling me I need one more cause five children are here," she explains, having already dropped in another quarter. A moment later she is in possession of her fifth prize.

"Let's go give Jesus's bounty to the children," she tells her son and he nods. They go from table to table allowing each child to select a prize. Mother and son give away all five prizes and leave smiling, pleased God's work has been done.

After being seated and finishing my meal, I make my way to the cashier. I notice on a vacated table that had not yet been cleaned a stuffed monkey playing a drum.

CHAPTER 3

KUDZU COMMUNION

When I first noticed that kudzu, I said to myself, "Millie, spray that stuff with Roundup before it takes over." Well, I let it slip my mind and it grew and grew. Now look at it. He's right there. You can see him just by looking. Jesus on the cross. This isn't like those people who see Jesus in grilled cheese sandwiches or potato chips. Oh no, this is Jesus making his presence felt. Like Jesus says in the Gospel of John, "I am the true vine." He didn't say, "I am the grilled cheese sandwich" or "I am the big potato chip." Just look at it. It's a good thing I didn't spray Jesus with Roundup. God only knows how deep down in hell I might have gone.

NO MORE

No more, dear Lord, can I have you so near.
Away, take now the splintered cross I bear.
No longer, Lord, tangle me in steadfast fear.
How, please tell, what you ask of me is fair?
When shadows darken, you are never there.
Alone, I tremble, stare, pray for insight.
Words do not heal, nor keep the Lord aware.
I try to keep you, Lord, with me at night.
My body, holy host to what lies within,
Is soon to cease and turn to deathly dust,
A fate you cast and left in the cold wind.
Still weak and weary, spiritless, I must
Believe, cruel Lord, more now the end is clear
When faith takes leave, Godless, I hold my fear.

CHAPTER 3

CHURCH GOING

1.

I love my Sunday mornings, so much so that sometimes I can't wait until Sunday and I go to Wednesday night Bible study. Doing that on Wednesday is hard for me with the kids and all, but I never miss a Sunday. Reverend Allen is the best pastor you're ever going to find. He starts out slow and then he builds and builds until he has the whole congregation calling out hallelujah and shouting praise to the Lord. I've never seen anyone inspire folks like he does. And the hymns! The precious Lord takes my hand when the choir is singing, and when Kayla does her solos, you can bet that there'll be tears in my eyes. After the service, I feel like a new woman. I feel the presence of the Lord Jesus in me, and I'm ready to face whatever might come my way in the week ahead.

Not only does Reverend Allen know how to preach a good sermon, he is there when you need him. When my mom was so sick, he'd come to the house and lead us in prayer. That meant so much to my mom. She would cheer up when she knew he was coming. And on the day she died, I was holding one of her hands and he was holding the other. He has a way of making you feel calm in times of trouble. He's such a good man. I've seen him reach in his own pocket when someone from the church was in need. He truly does the Lord's work, always putting others before himself.

The church is a place that fills my spiritual needs and it's a place where I can be with my people, people who share my beliefs and people who face the same things I do. It's my safe space, where I can be with my brothers and sisters. Sometimes people will try to take that away, like what that man did to those poor people in that Charleston church, but nothing can keep us away from where we feel at home, where we can be with each other and sing our praises to the Lord. They can try to shoot us and burn us out, but they can't break our spirit. They can't keep us from the strength we find in Jesus.

2.

My Dad left the Greek Orthodox Church when he married my Mom and promised to raise the kids in the church of my mother's upbringing. He kept to his word and became a lifelong member of the Methodist Church, giving more than his fair share and serving as church treasurer for over twenty years. I'm not sure why, but Mom stopped attending. Dad, though, carried on his promise alone, dragging the three kids to church every Sunday until we hit our teen years and put up too much resistance. Sleeping in always seems more appealing than hard pews. Dad continued to go every Sunday and would announce on Saturday nights, "I'll be leaving for church at 9:15 if anyone wants to come with me." Most of the time, we would beg off, but, on occasion, we would attend just to be with him.

As a child, church seemed to be a place for adult talk and for children to be still. I remember many Sunday mornings, when my legs that were too short to reach the floor, I would swing them back forth, letting them go under my seat and swing forward, stopping just short of the pew in front of me, just short enough to make my Dad afraid I'd hit it and disturb the people in front of us. "Be still," he would say. I can see myself wearing those uncomfortable clothes, the kind of garments that would make you squirm because everything seemed too tight and stiff. All that money in the collection plate would move around the congregation. I wanted to take some, but knew I couldn't. Instead, I'd add a dollar to the pile that my Dad had given me for my contribution. When the last hymn came, I was joyous, not because I had been elevated into some spiritual realm, but because soon it would all be over. After the minister would walk down the center aisle and the light would shine in the church through the front door, I knew I only had to shake the minister's hand before I would be free.

Somehow I managed to learn something about Methodist doctrine. There was a time when I could recite the books of the Bible, Old and New Testament, in order. I still have a few Bible verses memorized and know a good many Biblical stories. I understand the meaning of communion, the significance of religious holidays, and usually recognize the names of Biblical figures. I learned that the

Bible was a holy book that held the teachings of Christ, that Jesus died for our sins, and that I was headed to either heaven or hell, depending upon the choices I made. I accepted all of this without question and without much conviction. It was just there, like a clock or a chair might be.

After graduating high school, I applied to Southern Methodist University and was accepted. I knew I had to decide on a major, and given that "Methodist" was in the school's name, I considered becoming a minister. It seemed like a pleasant job. Give a speech once a week, conduct wedding services, baptize a baby now and then, and visit with people who weren't doing well. But even at the early age of eighteen, I felt I should have a deep belief in my religion if I were to become a minister. My decision to major in sociology rather than ministry was solidified when in my first semester I took a History of the Bible class, perhaps the class that had the greatest influence on me of any undergraduate or graduate course I've ever taken. Learning how the King James version of the Bible came to be, how years passed before stories were recorded, how translations from language to language changed what was included, how church leaders and political figures influenced what was and was not incorporated into what was called the word of God was more than enough to shake the little faith I had into pure skepticism. I felt as if what I had learned as a child was nothing but lies.

I drifted further and further from the church until my wife and I had a child and decided that some religious education was in order. If for no other reason, we agreed, she'll be a better reader of literature. We settled on the Unitarian Universalist for the purposes of indoctrinating our daughter. It's a church built on tolerance, open to all forms of spirituality, except those that propagate intolerance. It felt like a happy fit for our liberal views. We attended until our daughter decided in her teen years she'd rather sleep in than sit in hard pews. We have seldom gone back, but every now and then, we agree that we should return to that once-a-week time to reflect, to think about what it means to live a good life, to become a better person.

3.

I can't imagine what's wrong with those people. It's one thing if they want to pair up like that, but it's quite another for them to come to our church and tell us we don't know how to read the Bible. It's clear as can be that homosexuality is a sin, right there in the Bible. And they say we should let them get married in our church if they want to. I can't believe the nerve, telling us what we should believe. I'm glad our minister stood up to them. He explained how we love the sinner, but not the sin, and that they were welcome to stay as long as they respected our beliefs. And then they went on about how denying them their rights was disrespectful. I don't see why they couldn't go to some church that would allow them to be the sinners that they are. Why they wanted to push their way of being on us is beyond my comprehension.

That's why I sent a check to those people who refused to do a wedding cake for those homosexuals. It's not right that the gays are trying to force their lifestyle on others. I feel for those poor people who run that bakery—they're just trying to be good people, to follow their religious beliefs. The gays, though, they're only happy when you accept their sick ways. I tell you, I'll have no part of it, and I'm glad people in my church feel the same way.

CHAPTER 3

CHRISTIAN SPINOFFS

"Following an eye for an eye would soon turn everyone blind."

"Do unto others before they do unto you."

"On a hill far away stood an old rusted car, the emblem of capitalism and greed."

"Honor your Mother and Father until they are no longer worthy of being honored."

"Turn the other cheek if you want to be slapped again."

"If you think Leviticus is such a great moral guide, stone to death all those who commit adultery, or, if you prefer, sacrifice a lamb on the church altar next Sunday."

"In the beginning God created Adam and Eve in order to prove Darwin wrong."

"Thou shall not kill, unless you're (1) fighting for your country or (2) punishing someone who truly deserves it."

"Ask a biologist what would happen to you if you were swallowed by a whale."

"I wish Noah would have left behind these damn mosquitoes."

"Christ was a Jew so he is in part to blame for killing himself."

"Onward Christian Soldiers, under the sheets."

"Do this in remembrance of me: Lift your middle finger of you right hand and point it directly at yourself."

"Jesus wept because he took notice of you."

"Blessed are the children who have not been indoctrinated in your church."

"Praise be to the Pop Tart."

"And they hung Him on the cross, cha, cha, cha."

"Jesus loves the little children, some a little more than others."

"If the Lord was my shepherd, he'd gather my sheep, and I could just sit here on my fat ass."

"May the Lord go with you; you need to be watched."

"What a friend we have in Jesus; when he comes over, he always brings bread and wine."

"Holy Moly."

BODY TO BODY

Your grace guides my hand
when I hold the cross that hangs
around my neck, finger my rosary,
when I reach out to others,
cradle the helpless child, build shelter
for the homeless, feed the hungry.

Your grace guides my feet
when they walk with you,
even when blistered and raw, they follow
your path, move to be with you
on this pilgrimage toward salvation,
each step another step toward your glory.

Your grace guides my heart
when it beats in your rhythm,
beats with love, with compassion,
when it honors those who know
your ways, your gentleness, your kindness,
your forgiveness of our sins.

Your grace guides my eyes
when I see you on the cross, sacrificing
for others, blood coming from your palms,
your feet, taking on their pain, looking
down from that torturous tree
with God's crown of thorns.

Your grace guides my mouth
when I remember you in silent
communion, bread, blood red wine,
that lets me take you in,
lets me be with you,
my body a part of your body.

CHAPTER 3

JUDGMENT

My sister said on the witness stand her child was just under bad influences. She didn't think irreparable damage had been done. She still loved him. A Christian always forgives. A Christian doesn't judge.

That fourteen year old child she loves tried to kill her. After his father went to jail for cutting her throat, he tried to finish the job. Shot her. He's smug, just like his Father. He sat in that courtroom, giving her the evil eye. She would smile and he would look away as if my sister did him wrong.

It's hard to tell your sister her child is no good. I've tried. But she insists that everyone has an angel in them. They just need to find their white cloud.

That boy has been a bad storm since he was born. She never sees a thing or her seeing is with eyes I don't have. Lightning lights the night for blind love.

She can't cover that scar around her neck with her cross. She can't let that evil boy do her more harm. She can't live in the eye of God's tornado.

PRIEST CONFESSES

My intentions, I believe,
were pure.
I'd see her
working the street.
I'd say:
"The doors of the Church
are always open."
She'd smile,
so innocently
you'd think she was one
of God's angels.
"Thank you, Father."
It became our ritual,
our liturgy.
She's young,
not yet hardened
like the others.
Delicate.
I prayed for her.
With each bead of my rosary,
she'd rush into my eyes—
adjusting her top
revealing
enough to entice,
cocking
her head, leaning
in the window of a car,
coming in.
I saw the Holy Mother
in her small face.
The night it happened
she broke our incantation.
"Would you like to take me there?"
"Yes."

CHAPTER 3

I thought she wanted
to confess, wanted
my help, wanted
to find her way.
"It will cost you fifty,
just like the others."
I reached
for my wallet.
I was confused.
She slid in right
next to me, ran
her hand
down my leg.
I placed the money
in her other hand.
She kissed my cheek,
my lips, then moved
her head
between my legs.
When the sirens sounded,
I was caught,
in communion
with the flesh
of Christ.

FOLLOWING GOD'S LAW

I could not give them God's money. When they talked of their hunger, I reminded them of the hunger of the soul. Yes, I was concerned with their health, but one's spiritual health is what matters. I take comfort knowing that my son rests with God. We did not succumb to the devil's temptation. God's tithings have not been touched. We did not yield to the yearnings of the flesh.

I miss my son and pray my daughter will be well, but I have no regrets. My soul is pure. God leads the way. I look to Him for guidance. His laws are laws. They must be followed. So you can understand that when the Church says to give your fair share, you give your fair share. The money I had was God's, not mine. I could not spend it on my own family. I prayed our nourishment would be found in our faith, that God would sustain us, see us through. Our problem was that our faith was not strong enough. We did not trust in the Lord as fully as we might.

Now, you come with your laws saying we did wrong. I say we did not do enough of what God says is right. You claim I killed my son by refusing to feed him. I say I fed him full of God's love and God's grace.

CHAPTER 3

A CHRISTIAN EDUCATION

Bob looked up from his brochure on wine vacations when Lily returned to the living room and asked, "Did you get her down?"

"Yes, she's finally asleep."

"Good. Thanks for doing that," Bob said, glad it wasn't his turn to do bedtime duties.

"I want to tell you, Bob, what Sarah asked me after school today," Lily said, sitting down next to Bob and taking his hand. Bob placed the brochure to his side. "She said, 'What does 'bitch' mean?' When I asked where she heard that, she said some of the girls were calling each other 'bitch.' I told her it was a bad word that some people use to describe women when they are acting mean, but it's not a word we would use."

"It sounds like you handled it well," Bob replied, squeezing her hand. "I guess she is at that age when she'll be hearing such things."

"I guess so. It made me wonder, though, if that school is a good place for her. So many rough kids go there," Lily said, coding more in the word "rough" than she would ever acknowledge. "I'm not sure if I want to expose Sarah to all that."

"That's part of growing up, learning about those things." The image of his beautiful little Sarah rushed into his thoughts as he spoke. So innocent, so sweet, he thought, and he flinched a little at his own words.

"I guess, but I don't think we want her growing up just yet. She's only six-years-old." It was as if Sarah knew what was really in his mind.

"Was she upset or anything after you told her what bitch meant?" Bob wanted to know.

"No, she didn't say any more about it," Lily reported, but then added, "It's not just that. It's that whole environment."

"I know what you mean," Bob said, implying what he would not say out loud. "We like her teacher though. That's something."

"Yes, it is. She's very caring, and she knows how to handle her problem kids. They take a lot of her time." Lily saw Sarah's class, Ms Andrews bending over to help one child while the other twenty-nine were left on their own. The image of mostly brown and black children came to her, a few white ones. All were unkempt, acting up. "I wonder if we should consider an alternative school," she said.

Bob felt the weight of her suggestion, and after a moment, responded, "Given where we live, I don't think we have too many alternatives." They lived in a small university town which was big enough to offer one of everything, but not big enough to give an abundance of choices. "You're not thinking about quitting your job and home schooling her, are you?" Bob blurted out, afraid how Lily might answer.

"No, we need our two incomes. That wouldn't work," Lily said and Bob breathed more easily. He enjoyed the luxuries their two salaries gave them. Lily worked in real estate and Bob sold insurance for State Farm, and with both their earnings, they could afford just about everything a small town might offer.

"We might consider that Christian school on Warren Street," Lily added. "I've heard it isn't too expensive, and it's close to where we live and, most importantly, she would be getting a Christian education, and she would be away from that situation she's in."

"It's Lutheran affiliated, isn't it? Evangelical, right?" Bob asked, pretty sure he knew the answer. Bob considered himself a man of faith, but his beliefs did not align with the ideas of Evangelical Christians.

"Yes, I think so, but the curriculum is basically the same, except they have a Bible class," Lily replied.

Bob was beginning to wonder if Lily was already committed to this possibility. "We're Presbyterian, not Evangelical Lutheran."

"I know that, but I don't think learning about the Bible would hurt her," Lily offered.

"How would you feel if she brought home a picture of a little Christian family riding dinosaurs, or if she learned that your brother was going to hell because he has a same-sex partner?" Bob said.

"That wouldn't make me happy," Lily replied.

"That's what scares me about such schools," Bob went on. "Literal readings of the Bible lead to crazy ideas. I rather Sarah hear the word 'bitch' than be taught such things."

CHAPTER 3

    Lily sat still for a moment. She knew she felt the same way Bob did. She allowed herself to think that might be an option because she was unhappy with Sarah's situation, but she knew such schools are more interested in teaching fundamentalist beliefs than giving children a solid educational foundation. Much of what they believe, Sarah thought, Bob and I don't accept.

    "You're right," Lily finally said. "I don't want that for Sarah either. But I don't like where she is now. I want her safe. I want to protect her from the world."

    "Me too. I guess no parent can protect a kid every second from what the world serves up."

    "I wish that school had nicer kids for Sarah to play with," Lily said, and then she added after a moment, "I guess we'll have to leave her where she is."

    "It's a shame that our church doesn't run a school," Bob offered.

    "I wish it did," Lily agreed, "I'd send Sarah there in a second. She'd be with kids like her. Nice kids."

    "We'll teach Sarah what's right, protect her with our love, our guidance," Bob said, feeling a sense of responsibility.

    "That's what we'll do," Lily sighed.

    "It's hard to be a good Christian, to lead a child in the right direction," Bob said.

    "Yes, it is," Lily agreed and they both nodded.

PRAYERS

1.

Jesus, I think my neighbor was just beating his wife. I heard them arguing and then I heard her crying out for him to stop. It's quiet now, but I know what I heard. I'm sure he was hitting her. My wife says I shouldn't get involved. She says that if I do, I'll put our whole family at risk. I have to admit that the man frightens me too. Help me, Jesus. I don't know what I should do.

2.

This is Myra, God. I know I haven't prayed as much as I should have and when I did, it wasn't for anything real important. But this time, it's real serious. You see, my Mom is real sick and I'm hoping you can help her get better. She's been in the hospital for a long time now, and I really want her to get better and come home. I miss her so bad, God. You don't need her up in heaven with you like I need her here. I need her real bad. I really do. So please, please, please, God, let my Mom get better.

3.

Dear God, keep me from pushing those keys again. With four quick strokes, I'm there, with all those naked women doing everything imaginable. They seem to be calling to me, calling me in, saying look at what we're doing now. You don't want to miss it, do you? I try not to listen to them, but they keep calling, God. Tell them to stop. Tell them to stop doing those things.

4.

It's me again, Lord, with my nightly pray. I ask you to look over my family. Keep them healthy, particularly the little ones. Help Paul and Maggie through their troubles. I know Paul can be pig-headed, like his father, but he is a good man. Help all my little grandbabies grow up strong and with You by their sides. Help my brother Gerry find the love to forgive his daughter. She was just born that way. And help everyone in my family to be kind to each other. Amen. Oh, I almost forgot. Thank you for helping Sarah through her operation. She's doing fine now. Amen again.

5.

Thank you, Jesus, for sparing my family when that tornado hit. We need your help now. We got nothing left. There's nothing but an empty lot where our house once was. We lost everything but the shirts on our backs. The tornado even wrecked our truck. I got $7.00 in my wallet. I got nothing to feed my kids. We got nothing. Tell you the truth, I don't know why I'm praying. This prayer ain't worth a thing. What kind of God would take away everything. We got nothing.

6.

I'm counting my blessings, Lord. Thank you for giving me such a long life and letting Jimmy be with me for so many years before you took him away. Thank you for blessing me with three beautiful children and five beautiful grandchildren and one beautiful great grandchild. Thank you for giving my family the ambition to work for their money so they don't have to live like those people across town. And thank you for making us all good people. Amen.

7.

Oh God. Let me get through this.

8.

I kneel before You, Holy Father, to ask for your hand to guide me as I lead this congregation. These are hard working people who have lived through many troubles, but have kept their faith in You. Help me on this Sunday morning be a passage way for them to embrace Your Glory. Amen.

9.

I'm sitting here in your church, Jesus, wondering if I am a true believer. The minister keeps quoting the Bible, calling it the Holy Scriptures, but all I can think about is how that Bible was written. Put together long after you walked this earth. Put together over the centuries. Put together by those who wanted to impose their beliefs. Translated over and over from one language to another. It's hard for me to accept that King James got your teachings down right. There is so much stupid stuff in there. Maybe I should I stop thinking about it. That's what faith is all about, right? Just believing. Giving yourself over. I'm not sure if I can do that. Maybe I'm a hypocrite for being here. Maybe I shouldn't come back.

10.

The nuns keep telling me that I should be like the Virgin Mary until I'm married. But Danny keeps telling me that he wants us to show our love for each other, and I really do love him. We can't get married yet because we're too young. So, Jesus, this is my question: If I let Danny do what he wants to do, will I burn in hell for eternity? I'd appreciate it, Jesus, if you'd give me a sign one way or the other. Please hurry with your answer because Danny and I are going out this coming Friday night.

11.

Cancer. My cross to carry. I don't know why, God, you've given me this burden, but I trust in your infinite wisdom. Help me be strong, particularly for Steve and, the love of my life, my little Jenny. Amen

12.

Heavenly Father, we join these two, Sarah and Camille, in holy matrimony. May Your blessings follow them throughout their days. May they live in health and prosperity and know the wisdom of Your teachings. Amen.

13.

Forgive me, God, for saying my silly prayer—Father, Son, and Holy Ghost, whoever eats the fastest gets the most—in front of grandma at dinner. She said I had to come in here to pray for Your forgiveness. So I guess I'm sorry, but I still think it is kind of funny. Amen.

14.

Oh my God! Oh my God! That car just ran off the road into that ditch! May God help them. I can't believe it. Oh my God!

15.

Save us Lord. We've been in this bunker for two hours now. The rockets haven't stopped. They just keep coming. They're hitting all around us. This bunker couldn't take a direct hit. No one is talking. We're just sitting, our backs against the wall. There's five of us in here. We're all praying. Damn, there's another one. Another one. God, help us get out of this shit hole.

THE TRICK

I must admit I'm pretty skeptical about life after death. Maybe we live on in some kind of chemical or spirit form, but I can't buy the story of heaven and hell. Heaven and hell are fictions to make us feel better about dying and to keep us in line. Jesus was probably just a guy who knew a few tricks. Over time, people exaggerated what he did and turned it into a religion. That's how we got the New Testament. It offers some good principles to live by, but, for the most part, it's nothing but a fabrication, just like all the other holy books in the world. People seem to need myths to explain things, particularly when it comes to the afterlife. They want to believe that their time on earth is not all there is. It makes for a good story, but that's all it is, a story.

"Well, if you don't believe, where do you think we came from?" people will say. That always strikes me as a stupid question. There are some pretty good biological explanations. If you try to present those facts, they will quickly add, "And where do you think all that came from?" Then I'll say, "Where do you think God came from?" "He always was," they say. Then I try either, "Yes, he 'always was,' after we made him up" or "I can say the same thing about biological combinations that led to human life," but that's where the conversation ends. It becomes a matter of belief—who has the most convincing story. Theologians have a more comforting tale. It's just hard for me to accept their account.

Most people get upset when I say stuff like this, so most of the time I keep my thoughts to myself. If they want to believe, that's fine. I just wish they wouldn't try to impose their beliefs on everyone else. That's where all the trouble starts. They think they have the one true way, that all others are sinners, and that they're doing God's work by spreading the word. This is the kind of thinking that has led to the most brutal, violent, and oppressive acts humans have done to each other. I don't like to think of what's been done in the name of Christianity or any other religion for that matter.

CHAPTER 3

The trick is to lead a good life. It doesn't matter whether or not God exists. If you lead a good life, you're set because you've led a good life, done the things a good Christian might do. If God doesn't exist, then you can take pride in the life you've led. You would've been the kind of person you wanted to be.

YOU CAN'T BOO JESUS

CHARACTERS:

John, male, age 28, in a six-month-old relationship with Mary
Mary, female, age 26, in a six-month-old relationship with John

SETTING:

Park bench following an Easter parade.

AT RISE:

John, sitting on bench, shaking his head.

JOHN

You can't boo Jesus. That's just not right.

MARY

No one was booing Jesus. They were booing that poor, pathetic guy playing Jesus.

JOHN

He was carrying the cross.

MARY

But the cross looked like it was made of Styrofoam and he was carrying it under his arm. He was wearing white pants and a white hoodie and his beard was falling off. That isn't the picture I have in my mind of Jesus carrying the cross.

JOHN

All that is beside the point.

MARY

This guy was just walking along instead of being in an Easter parade. I'm surprised everyone wasn't laughing.

JOHN

You can't laugh at Jesus. That's not right either.

MARY

Don't you think this guy was funny, in a sad kind of way?

JOHN

No, this is not funny at all. It's about respect.

MARY

God gave us a sense of humor, John. Lighten up.

JOHN

Are you telling me not to take my faith seriously?

MARY

No, I'm telling you that this guy was doing such a poor job of portraying Jesus that it was funny.

JOHN

Even if he was doing a poor job, he was still portraying Jesus and people shouldn't boo or laugh.

MARY

John, you're being ridiculous.

JOHN

You might call it ridiculous, but I see it as being a good Christian.

MARY

This isn't a question of who is a better Christian.

JOHN

I think it is. A good Christian wouldn't boo or laugh.

MARY

Who made you the grand arbiter of all things? Judge not…

JOHN

I must follow the principles of my faith; otherwise I'm not a true Christian. I can't just follow my faith only when it's easy for me.

MARY

I don't think it says anywhere in the Bible that you can't boo a fake Jesus.

JOHN

It's about honoring the name, honoring Him.

MARY

You have too many rules, John. Christianity is a religion of love, of joy.

JOHN

Who's being the judge now?

MARY

I'm not judging. I'm only telling you what I believe.

JOHN

Well, I guess we believe different things.

MARY

I guess so.

JOHN

That makes me sad.

MARY

Me too.

JOHN

I don't think there is anything we can do about it.

MARY

I think you're right.

JOHN

I guess this is it.

CHAPTER 3

                    MARY
I think you're right again.
                    JOHN
I thought you could have been the one.
                    MARY
I guess not.
                    JOHN
Good luck to you.
                    MARY
For some reason, I want to boo.

CHAPTER 4

CRIMINAL TALES

THE DRUGSTORE HEIST

On a slow Saturday morning, Genie, age ten, and Ronnie, age eight, decided they would hit the drugstore. Their goal was to get as many toys as possible without getting caught. "Look," Genie said, "I know this store. I've been there plenty of times. They got a whole aisle of neat stuff."

"What kind of stuff?" Ronnie wanted to know.

"You know, lots of things—Duncan yo-yos, Matchbox cars, all kinds of stuff," Genie replied, grabbing a piece of paper and beginning to draw in pencil the layout of the drugstore. "Here's the front door where we'll go in," he said, continuing to fill the page as he talked. "There's a check-out counter right next to it. Someone is always working there," he noted, reaching for his box of colored pencils. He drew a colorful picture of a woman in a flowery dress standing behind the counter. "I'll start talking with her to cover you while you go get as many things as you can fit in your pockets. Got it?" Genie began to sketch the toy aisle with shelves full of loot.

Genie must know what he's talking about, Ronnie thought. He's a lot older than I am. Ronnie was also persuaded by the quality of Genie's drawing. "She won't be able to see me?" Ronnie asked, pointing to the woman with long yellow hair that Genie had colored. Ronnie liked the nice smile and red lips Genie gave her.

"No, I'll be keeping her busy and you'll be in this aisle here, aisle three."

"What should I get?" Ronnie remembered that sometimes it was hard for him to decide what to buy when faced with all the choices a toy display presents. He was hoping Genie would give him a shopping list.

CHAPTER 4

"Small stuff. You won't be able fit anything big in your pockets," Genie reasoned and Ronnie felt that would help him narrow down the choices. "You'll have to act fast. So just grab what you can. Okay?"

"Okay," Ronnie said, beginning to see the whole plan unfold. Genie put the finishes touches on his drawing and they began the two block journey to the drugstore. "What do I do after I fill all my pockets?"

"You walk out the front door," Genie advised. "Walk slow like nothing has happened. We'll meet at this tree." Genie stopped and tapped the large oak tree they were passing. "Got it?"

"Yeah, I'll meet you here," Ronnie agreed.

"Take your shirt out of your pants. That will hide all the things you get." Ronnie did what he was told, glad that Genie was thinking of everything. "When we meet up, we'll split up the stuff. Half for you and half for me," Genie said.

Ronnie nodded, taking it all in.

When they arrived outside the drugstore, they checked with each other to make sure they were both ready. They entered. Genie went straight to the check-out counter and Ronnie, remembering Genie's drawn floor plan, went to the third aisle, but he didn't see any toys. He walked down the aisle to make sure the toys weren't there. No toys. He looped around to the fourth aisle and there they were, toy after toy, ready for the taking. He walked the whole aisle deciding what to take. He saw lots of possibilities. He decided to peek around the corner of the aisle to see if Genie was keeping the woman, who didn't look much like Genie's drawing of her, busy, but he saw the automatic doors opening as Genie walked into the sunlight. Ronnie knew he had to act quickly. He went straight to several things he saw on his walk down the aisle. Miniature dinosaurs, soap bubbles, cat's-eye marbles, eight pairs of dice, several little cars but not the good Matchbox kind, a small box of crayons, and a couple of party whistles all found their way into Ronnie's pockets. Keeping in mind Genie's advice, he walked slowly to the front door, took one step out, and then felt a strong hand grab his arm. "Come with me," a man dressed in a white lab coat said. The pharmacist had been watching Ronnie snatch the toys. He led Ronnie to the back of the store and told him to empty his pockets. Ronnie placed one item after another on the counter. After he put the dinosaurs there, it looked like they were standing guard.

"What is your name and what is your telephone number?" the pharmacist said in a stern voice. Ronnie, too frightened to do anything else but comply, gave him the information. "You stay right here," the pharmacist ordered, as he moved toward the phone. Ronnie watched, knowing the pharmacist was calling his mom. He could not hear what was being said, but after a few minutes he returned. "Do you know what you did is wrong?" the pharmacist asked. Ronnie nodded yes. "Your mother assures me that she will deal with you. You can go now, but don't come back in my store unless you are with one of your parents. I won't have you stealing from me again." Ronnie was frozen in place, not sure if the pharmacist was finished his lecture. He thought the dinosaurs might attack. He didn't move until pharmacist said, "Go on, get out of here," and then he ran for the door as if the dinosaurs as well as the pharmacist's final words were chasing him.

Outside, Ronnie was shaking as he started walking toward the oak tree where he was supposed to rendezvous with Genie. Before he got there, Genie came running up. "What did you get?"

"I didn't get anything. I got caught," Ronnie mumbled.

"What happened?"

"I had all this stuff and this man caught me. He called my mom and made me give back all the things I had," Ronnie said, and in that moment, he felt something in his back pocket. He reached in and found an unopened bag of marbles. A horror rushed over him. He thought he had placed everything with the dinosaurs. He did not want to be in possession of stolen goods. He spotted a gutter. He raced there without saying a word, knelt at its open mouth, and tossed the marbles down.

"Why did you do that?" Genie asked.

"I don't want them," Ronnie answered. "Why didn't you keep talking with the woman at check-out?"

"I ran out of things to say," Genie answered.

"The toys are on the fourth aisle, not the third."

"I thought it was the third," Genie said, sounding truly sorry he had given Ronnie the wrong information.

"I have to go home. I have to find out what my punishment will be. I bet my mom won't let us play together anymore," Ronnie said, thinking that would be one of the consequences he could easily accept.

WOMAN CHARGED

Fawns are so cute. I just added a touch.
I was taking good care of her. Put her
in my car when she was hurt, wrapped
her wound, gave her blankets for the ride.
I kept her in the yard while I nursed her
back to health. She learned to take food
from my hand. She would come running
when I opened the gate. Her eyes grew
soft with appreciation, took me in.

Then, I just couldn't give her up.
I didn't think one pair of zircon-studded
earrings would cause such a fuss.
I can't believe that I'm being charged
with illegally possessing a wild animal.
They let those hunters shoot them
but I can't dress one up a bit for the holidays.
They say it's animal cruelty. What's cruel
is not knowing how you might be called,

how you have to go to them. This brown
coloring on my face and these long lashes
made her feel more at ease. I'd wear the skins
so we could hide behind those few trees.
I only wore the antlers one time. Stomping
and kicking up the dirt must be what got
my neighbor's attention. That's when
she called the police, that's when I saw
my baby's little wound begin to bleed.

CHAPTER 4

MAN ORDERED

1.

I saw it coming,
that hand,
that once stroked
my face
soft-like,
that shook
holding mine,
that slid deep
down there,
as he begged
for more of me
until I was afraid.

I saw it coming.
and I went
dead cold,
like ice
ready to crack.

I saw it coming
when Daddy hit Momma
regular,
like a clock,
and Momma's face
was broken.

I saw it coming,
large and angry,
down
across my eyes,
blocking out
the light.

I saw
after the judge said
we should marry
with a ring.

2.

I said I wanted
to do right,
but to have to marry her
would ruin what I got.
I said I'd marry her
if I had to
just to keep from jail.
Judge said,
"Son, you promise
to do right by her?"
"I'll do right by her,"
I told him,
"I'll do her right."

CHAPTER 4

THE INTERVIEW

CHARACTERS:

Reporter: Male, age 32, ambitious journalist
Prisoner: Male, age 38, convicted murderer

SETTING:

Small room within a prison, furnished with only a table and two chairs.

AT RISE:

Reporter enters room, carrying a satchel. The prisoner is already seated.

REPORTER

Thank you for agreeing to meet with me. *(Sits and takes out a writing pad and pen and then places his satchel on the floor beside him.)*

PRISONER

No problem. I don't have much else to do.

REPORTER

As I told you, I think your case is an interesting one, and I'd like to do a story about it from your perspective. So, if you still agree, I'd like to ask you some questions.

PRISONER

Go right ahead.

REPORTER

You've admitted to killing twelve men. What made you stop? What made you turn yourself in?

PRISONER

I knew if I didn't turn myself in, I'd kill again. I didn't want to keep killing.

REPORTER

What made you want to kill? How did this start for you?

PRISONER

The first time I killed someone I surprised myself. It was about 10:30 at night, and I was getting into my car at Wal-Mart. I heard this guy yelling at his wife—I assumed it was his wife—he was cursing her out, telling her she spent too much money. She got in their car and he was still yelling at her. She kept saying, "We got to eat. We got to eat." Then he started hitting her. That's when I decided to do it. I took my gun out my glove compartment, walked right up behind him, and shot him dead.

REPORTER

Did you think you were helping her?

PRISONER

Yeah. I thought I was helping her, helping all of us. That son-of-a-bitch deserved to die. He lost his right to exist when he started hitting that poor woman.

REPORTER

Did it ever occur to you that maybe she didn't want him dead?

PRISONER

As time went on, such thoughts came to me, particularly after I'd taken out some asshole and the woman he was hurting would be on the news crying, saying how much she loved the person I had just killed. I killed for the women. I even saw a couple of women saying they were sorry I killed their pimp. It just goes to show you how a man can mess up a woman's mind. I still believe that the women were better off without the assholes I killed. They just needed a little time to realize it.

REPORTER

So you always thought you were helping some woman who was being mistreated by some guy.

PRISONER

Yeah. That's right. I ended the life of this miserable creep who was shouting at women when they went in and out of an abortion clinic.

CHAPTER 4

That's a tough time for a woman, trying to decide what they want to do, and they didn't need some guy yelling all these vile things when they went by. I went to AA meetings, had to pretend I had a drinking problem, to listen to the stories these guys would tell about what they did to their wives and girlfriends. You wouldn't believe what some of these people would blame on alcohol—sure, alcohol had an influence, but they were to blame for their actions. Two or three of the people I killed I found that way.

REPORTER

How else did you select your victims?

PRISONER

I'd read the paper, the crime reports, to find targets. I search them out and then put a stop to what they were doing. One time I just struck up a conversation with this guy in the mall. You'd be surprised what he told me, a complete stranger, about his wife. He was bitching and bitching about how his wife was making him sit there while she went off shopping. She was probably buying stuff for his stupid ass. Then he starts talking about how she let herself go, gained some weight, so he hooked up with this other woman on the side. He said she really knows how to take care of a man and then gives me a little wink. I think it was the wink that made me decide he had to go. He was so smug about it.

REPORTER

But after killing twelve men, you decided you shouldn't kill anyone else. Right? That's when you turned yourself in?

PRISONER

Yeah. I decided an even dozen should be enough to send men a message, even though I now realize there are still lots of men who still don't get it. Like you, for example. What are you doing to your wife that could earn you a place on my "lesson learned" list?

REPORTER

I'm not married.

PRISONER

But you were married at one time?

REPORTER

Yes, but we both agreed to go our separate way.

PRISONER

So what did you do to her to make her want to go her separate way?

REPORTER

Nothing, really. Let's get the conversation back on track. This interview is about you, not me.

PRISONER

That's what I mean. Some guys just don't get it.

REPORTER

What do you think I'm missing?

PRISONER

Given that you are a man who works with words, I bet you could talk circles around your ex, make her think she was always the one in the wrong, make her feel she was always to blame. You would act like you were the rational one and she was the crazy one because she would get frustrated with you. This is how things played out, isn't it?

REPORTER

She might agree with you, but that's not how I see it.

PRISONER

Of course it isn't.

REPORTER

Look, I don't have to justify myself to you. I haven't killed anyone.

PRISONER

That isn't the question. The question is if you deserve to be killed.

CHAPTER 4

> REPORTER

No, I don't.

> PRISONER

That's what every man I killed would say.

> REPORTER

I think this interview is coming to an end.

> PRISONER

Denial is a typical male strategy for the wrongs they've done. Confess. I have. What else did you do to her?

> REPORTER

I didn't do anything to her.

> PRISONER

Denial. Answer the question. Be accountable. That's why I killed twelve men, to make all men accountable.

> REPORTER

We had our differences, but I never did anything that would make me a candidate for murder.

> PRISONER

What did you do to her?

> REPORTER

There may have been some times when I said some things that were cruel, but…

> PRISONER

Okay, now we are getting somewhere. Verbal abuse. Sometimes that can feel worse than physical abuse to a woman.

> REPORTER

It wasn't verbal abuse.

PRISONER

What is your ex-wife's name?

REPORTER

Margaret. She went by Margo.

PRISONER

The question is if Margo felt it was verbal abuse. How many times did you cheat on her?

REPORTER

I don't have to answer these questions.

PRISONER

No, you don't, but I'm trying to help you see.

REPORTER

I know what I have and haven't done. I don't need your help.

PRISONER

So, you cheated on her. Probably had to tell quite a few lies about it. Do you know how hurtful that can be, particularly if you couple that with verbal abuse, try to make it seem like it's her fault.

REPORTER

You think you've got everything all figured out.

PRISONER

Not quite everything. One more question: When you were working on your "amicable" separation, were you thinking about who you would call when you were done with Margo?

REPORTER

What if I did?

CHAPTER 4

                    PRISONER

Then you would have earned your rightful place on my hit list. We would have established that you are a selfish bastard who is likely to do harm to women.

                    REPORTER

Oh, please.

                    PRISONER

Did Margo ever say to you that she could kill you for what you'd done?

                    REPORTER

That's just an expression.

                    PRISONER

I'll take that as a "yes," which means that Margo believes as I do that you merit a place on my list of those who deserve to die. My job was simply to carry out the actions women wanted done, but couldn't do themselves.

                    REPORTER

Who made you the judge of all things?

                    PRISONER

I listen for the evidence to build a case. I stand with the women as jurors. We decide who is guilty. Isn't that how the system works?

                    REPORTER

You're sick. (*Begins to gather his things. Reaches down for his satchel.*)

                    PRISONER

You wanted my perspective. Here it is. (*Lifts chair over his head, ready to strike the reporter as the reporter bends down to get his satchel. Blackout.*)

THE CRIMINAL MIND

I've had a mind:

> To take in some impulsive moment what wasn't mine, to slip in a pocket or under an arm some small object I decided I wanted to possess, even though I've always had the good fortune to be able to buy whatever I've needed or wanted. Perhaps I was seduced by the forbidden, by the thrill of the game, or by the something-for-nothing ease of the quick grab. Most of the time, I have resisted such temptations, kept myself from standing among thieves.

> To do harm with hands, fists, bats, knives, guns to others, when frustration moved to anger, when injury seemed to call for further injury, when by order or by instinct to defend. Always such thoughts, predicated on an understanding of physical pain and death, were strategies my body had for guarding its boundaries. Always, I've held back.

> To violate minor laws, the ones controlling vehicle traffic, the ones determining what substances at what age can be consumed, the ones legislating sexual behavior, the ones governing where you should dispose of your bodily and material waste, the ones guiding pedestrian movement, the ones …. Guilty.

> To plot unfortunate consequences for my enemies, to create schemes so devious and to utter words so cutting that my enemies would find themselves prostrate, powerless, desperate for a helping hand. My methods might be legal or not. Such plans always stayed in the world of fantasy, stayed short of execution because I was too afraid to act, because I didn't want to be that person.

> To cheat on taxes, on tests, on tales I've told, telling myself that everyone does such things, that everyone cuts corners, fudges a little, tells a little lie now and then, but not really believing

my own justifications, not accepting the things I have and have not done.

To betray people I love, to break oaths, to disregard promises, to discount commitments, most often for selfish reasons, most often without justification or much reflection, most often by careless neglect. I have been that person and it felt criminal.

FROM THE BRIDGE

1.

The dumb bitch hit my car. If she had been more careful, none of this would have happened. I was pissed, but I didn't want to do her any real harm. I just wanted to scare her. I bashed her hood with my car jack, and I was pulling the bitch out her car when her shirt ripped open so I just yanked some more and it came off. By that time she was out, and I got her skirt and then her bra. I heard them cheer. I just thought I'd teach her a lesson, teach her to be more careful. I never thought she'd jump in if she couldn't swim. I never knew she was such a stupid bitch. Now, I've got to pay 'cause she didn't have a fucking brain.

2.

The paper says we all cheered. Not all of us did. I know I didn't. Most of us got there after it started. We didn't know what was going on. I guess some cheered when he ripped her clothes off. I guess they thought that was funny. I guess they thought that he wouldn't hurt her, even though he had that iron pipe in his hand. I didn't cheer—he was coming at her, hitting her, backing her against the rail. When she jumped, he looked straight at us and said, "Good for that bitch." I thought: Yes! Good for her! She got away! Maybe I clapped then, let out some noise.

    We should have tried to stop him. We should have done something. I'd hate to think that the last thing she heard were those cheers.

3.

Lord, Lord, why didn't they help me? Couldn't they see what he was doing to me? Couldn't they see I'd done no wrong? Why did they cheer and cheer that wrong?

CHAPTER 4

RAILWAY SHOOTING

They put me on the stand to put him away, but he was defending himself. He accused me of being a coward because I held on to that woman. Said I used her as a shield when the shooting started. I took three bullets—one just below my belt, one in my leg, and one in my left arm—I thought I'd die from all the blood. It soaked my pants like I'd peed myself. It was warm, a strange comfort. The woman got shot too, just once in the shoulder. Six people were killed and nineteen of us wounded. The sounds were coming from that train—people were yelling, "Oh, my God!" Then the shots, the screams, the pleas, but everything seemed to go silent when he stood over me. He stared down, pointing that gun right at me. He looked at me like I deserved to be shot. The same look he gave me in court before the judge stopped him. Then he fired and the silence broke. "Are you alright? Are you alright?" she kept asking as we held on to each other like kids afraid of the dark. I couldn't answer. Couldn't speak. Words just wouldn't come out. Next thing I remember they were taking me away: "You'll be alright, buddy. Hang in there." And I'm thinking, this must be a movie. Then, with the pain, I passed out. It's been several months now. I'm doing much better, but I want to talk with that woman, tell her I didn't pee my pants, thank her for letting me hold on, for asking, like the judge, if I was alright.

CRIMES OF UNITED STATES POLITICIANS

A crime, when they lead us into war because it serves their donors, keeps the money flowing in their direction; when they claim to support the troops, but fail to provide adequate medical care; and when they pontificate on the Fourth of July, Veterans' Day, and Memorial Day about our brave, heroic soldiers and their sacrifices without once thinking about those who have been killed or wounded by their own political positioning.

A crime, when they impose their moral clichés on others, believing their way of seeing the world should be everyone's way of seeing the world; when they pretend to hold certain moral beliefs to accrue some political advantage; when they prove themselves to be hypocrites, doing what they preach against; and when they call on God to justify why everyone should not be equal under the law.

A crime, when they knowingly lie on behalf of their political party and their own self-interests; when they intentionally create political campaigns based in falsehoods and innuendo; when they misrepresent their positions as they move from one constituency group to the next, from one circumstance to another, from one person who might and one who might not vote for them; and when they are exposed for their own mendacity, they offer nothing more than more lies.

A crime, when they bargain away what they know is best for the people for promises of the next political cookie; when they keep the door shut to those who might have opposing ideas; when they surround themselves with sycophants, toadies that will only mirror their colors; and when they evoke "the will of the American people" without regard to the will of the American people.

A crime, when they pass laws designed to suppress voting, claiming fraud when virtually none exists; when they gerrymander boundaries so that political representation is no longer representative; when they sell out, bowing down before the most wealthy, in order to get campaign funds; and when they are willing to say or do anything to hold their position of power.

A crime, when they tell women that they know more about their bodies than they do; when they are willing to deny access to medical care for political gain; or when they refuse to vote in favor of equal pay for equal work; when they reject the possibility of reasonable maternity leave; when they patronize women, acting as if they need their protection; and when they kill under the name of pro-life.

A crime, when they muscle their way through international relations, threatening military might and economic chaos to those who are skeptical or suspicious of U.S. policy; when they prefer to bomb than negotiate, suggesting that they are the ones standing on moral ground; and when they shut their eyes to atrocities as long as those acts of violence don't carry perceived consequences for U.S. interests.

A crime, when they endorse legislation that allows the rich to get richer and the poor to become poorer; when they blame the poor for their hunger or homelessness without recognizing how the deck is stacked; when they vote against raising the minimum wage claiming it's bad for the American people as if the people who need the raise are not American people; and when they don't acknowledge that trickle-down economics is another way of saying piss on the majority of the people.

A crime, when they sacrifice the earth by relying upon their talking points; when they fund studies by paid lackeys who are told to find results to their liking, to deny and deny climate change; when they oppose laws designed to stop the pollution of our water and air; when they resist any effort for renewable fuels; and when they follow the requests of big oil for on and off-shore drilling, fracking, and pipelines, knowing that such practices are dangerous to our health and to the health of the earth.

A crime, when they obfuscate what they know science has proven, perhaps to pander to a misguided electorate, to appease companies deemed too important to the economy, or to build their campaign funds; when they doctor textbooks with false history and science; when they support charter schools as a means for eliminating public education; and when they decrease funding to education, turning education into a commodity only the rich can buy.

A crime, when they refuse to pass any legislation that would keep people, including innocent children, from being randomly murdered; when they pretend under rhetoric about the second amendment that we would all be safer if we each carried a gun; and when they allow the NRA to guide their actions and smile as their latest campaign fund swells; and when they don't mind if blood spills as long as they get to stay in office.

A crime, when they act like politicians, instead of people who care about the general good; when they forget that public service means to serve the public; when winning political advantage comes before the people; when they are willing to shut down needed services, destroy government agencies, and ruin individual lives in the name of ideological principles; and when they are surprised that few people hold politicians in high regard.

CHAPTER 4

TWIN

We spent sixty-eight years
together, two divided by two, tight
as a fist fighting off the terror
of separating from each other,
from our duplicate lives.
We couldn't escape, each
the other's exact exchange.
We couldn't forget, each
the other's irksome itch.
When I struck her,
I saw for the first time
another face, a fracture
in the mirror, a crack
that didn't reflect back.
When I struck her again,
she was alone, in pain,
her features twisted
like a knotted tree.
Torn apart as if lightening hit
we were two, ripped
down to the root, down
she on the floor, me
standing, iron in hand,
idiotic and free
as the blood running
from that stranger's head.

SHOTGUN MURDER

Probably wouldn't have done it, if I hadn't been drinking. Sometimes I drink a little too much. I know that. It seems like every time I get in some trouble, it's because of the booze. I guess I will quit if they put me in jail. I won't have no choice. My lawyer says it could be for six years. That don't seem right. A man should have some rights, even if he has been drinking. If that damn lawn mower worked right, it never would have happened. I had to keep stopping because it would give out. I'd cut a couple strips and it would stop—make this choking sound before it would quit on me. Each time I stopped to fix it, I took a little drink. I admit I got frustrated with that damn machine and that probably made me drink a little more. But after I had to stop maybe eight or nine times, you can't blame me for getting my shotgun and firing both barrels right in that engine. I didn't want that thing dying on its own any more. I wanted to kill it myself. My neighbor called the cops, told them I was drunk, shooting up things. But I only shot that lawn mower. It happened on my property. I should be able shoot it if I want. Cops said I broke the law—disorderly conduct while armed. A man should have some rights, should be able to shoot his own damn lawn mower, even if he had a few beers.

CHAPTER 4

RUINED DAY

I'm entitled
to justice,
to a new trial,
to a new lawyer.
There I was
on the stand
telling the jury
how it was,
how me and my friend
had sex
with that whore
and when she wanted her money,
I wouldn't give her none.
She kept saying,
"Give me my money,
give me my money,"
so I slapped her down
and when I saw she was scared,
that turned me on,
so I took out my knife.
She was really shaking then.
I wanted control,
I wanted to ruin her day,
not to hurt her.
It was so hot
I started stabbing her.
I couldn't stop.
Just when I was ready to explain
why it was that whore's fault,
my stupid bitch lawyer faints,
making me look bad.
She ruined my day
in court.
I got rights.

AN OPEN LETTER TO THE PERSON WHO BROKE INTO MY HOUSE

First, let me thank you for coming when I wasn't home. My guess is that neither of us wanted an encounter. We probably share that in common. I also appreciate the fact that you didn't cause much damage breaking in. It will be some hassle getting the window pane replaced, but that's much more easily done than replacing a doorframe. I must say, however, that while I am appreciative of how you went about your business in some regards, I was deeply saddened by the amount of your willful destruction throughout my house.

  I understand why you took the two televisions, the computer, and the golf clubs and why you swiped the cash and the jewelry you found, but did you really need to make such a mess? Given the looks of things, I imagine that you used the wedge or the driver from the golf clubs you took to smash up as much as you could. Those clubs, as I guess you discovered, would work best. Or maybe you randomly tossed things against walls or shattered them on the floor. I'm not sure about your methods. Some of the items you broke, I should mention, had sentimental value, like the candy dish I got when my grandmother died. I'm also sorry you demolished my mother's ceramic lamp. I know it wasn't the most attractive lamp ever created, but my mom made it for me when I moved into my first apartment. And did you need to pull books from the shelves? Surely you could tell that there was no hidden safe behind them. Didn't you think that would take too much time? The same goes for all the dishes you pulled from kitchen cabinets. Was it fun seeing how easily they broke on the tile floor? And pulling the ceiling fan down—that had to take some strength. Scooping ashes from the fireplace in the living room and dumping them all over the furniture seems a bit excessive as well. I should have cleaned out those ashes weeks ago.

  I wish too that instead of spraying messages to me in red paint on the walls you would have left me a note. You must have seen that there was plenty of paper next to the computer printer when you threw it to the floor. If you had to paint on the walls, however, I would have appreciated it if you had been more creative. Writing "fuck" and "suck me" in the bedroom and bathroom is unlikely to get you the desired results you are requesting. The drawing of the enormous penis from a technical perspective wasn't bad, but ultimately, rather banal. And peeing on the well-made bed was just crude, uncalled for really.

    I suppose I can see how doing such destruction would be fun, but I can't quite escape that it seems to me rather mean spirited. The house can be cleaned. Some of the items can be replaced. What I don't know is how I'm going to get rid of your presence, that lingering sense of meanness. It's a part of the house now. What you've taken, what you've destroyed is my comfort. It's hard to be here now, here in this place of villainy, of violence, of violation. I just thought you might want to know.

PAINTED BODY PARTS

When I opened the box, I thought it was a wall hanging. You know, an art deco thing, painted all gold and bright blue, one arm crossed over the other. I reached down to get a better look, started to lift it from its paper wrappings, but it didn't feel right. Too soft, like a sponge or rotten fruit, and there was that smell. I don't know why I didn't scream, but I didn't.

I knew what I had to do—I called the police. But as I waited, hoping they would soon arrive, I couldn't stop looking. Those limbs were resting there, still. The colors kept them, held them, displayed, fixed. I couldn't touch them again, but I took my umbrella, turned one arm, slowly, so I could see where it was cut off. Butchered. Clean. Smooth, like a pork chop. For a moment, I wanted it. I knew why he must have done it. I saw myself, knife and brush in hand.

CHAPTER 4

ON THE ONE-YEAR ANNIVERSARY OF FERGUSON

(The Ferguson anniversary marks the death of Michael Brown on August 9, 2014. The names included below are the names of the unarmed black men killed by police in the year following Brown's death. The list of names was compiled by *USA Today*, published on Monday, August 10, 2015.)

Black lives
reduced to a list,
date, name, age, locations

>August 11, 2014
>Ezell Ford, 25, Los Angeles, CA

>November 20, 2014
>Akai Gurley, 28, Brooklyn, NY

>November 22, 2014
>Tamir Rice, 12, Cleveland, OH

marking another year
that they're still killing us,
that black lives don't matter

>December 2, 2014
>Rumain Brisbon, 34, Phoenix, AZ

>December 30, 2014
>Jerame Reid, 36, Bridgeton, NJ

>January 30, 2015
>Artago Damon Howard, 36, Union County, AR

except to those who are black,
who know that those dead
are more than a date, name, age, and location

>February 4, 2015
>Jeremy Lett, 28, Tallahassee, FL

February 15, 2015
Lavall Hall, 25, Miami Gardens, FL

February 28, 2015
Thomas Allen, 34, Wellston, MO

more than another report to file away
more than an inconvenient detail to push aside
more than the latest public relations problem.

March 1, 2015
Charly Leundeu Keunang, 43, Los Angeles, CA

March 6, 2015
Naeschylus Vinzant, 37, Aurora, CA

March 6, 2015
Tony Robinson, 19, Madison, WI

They are flesh and blood reminders
of a broken system, of how the law of the land
doesn't apply, unless you happen to be white.

March 9, 2015
Anthony Hill, 27, DeKalb County, GA

March 12, 2015
Bobby Gross, 35, Washington, D.C.

March 19, 2015
Brandon Jones, 18, Cleveland, OH

They are flesh and blood reminders
of people who did nothing more than
drive with a busted brake light.

April 2, 2015
Eric Harris, 44, Tulsa, OK

April 4, 2015
Walter Scott, 50, North Charleston, SC

CHAPTER 4

> April 15, 2015
> Frank Shephard, 41, Houston, TX

They are flesh and blood reminders
of people who dared to ask a question,
who disagreed with the man in charge.

> April 22, 2015
> William Chapman, 18, Postsmouth, VA
>
> April 25, 2015
> David Felix, 24, New York, NY
>
> May 5, 2015
> Brendon Glenn, 29, Venice, CA

They are flesh and blood reminders
of people who drank a bit too much,
who declined to move on when told.

> June 15, 2015
> Kris Jackson, 22, South Lake Tahoe, CA
>
> June 25, 2015
> Spencer McCain, 41, Owings Mills, MD
>
> July 2, 2015
> Victor Emanuel Larosa, 23, Jacksonville, FL

They are flesh and blood reminders
of people who displayed their open hands
and their hands were declared a gun.

> July 12, 2015
> Salvao Ellswood, 36, Plantation, FL
>
> July 17, 2015
> Albert Joseph Davis, 19, Orlando, FL
>
> July 17, 2015
> Darrius Stewart, 19, Memphis, TN

They are flesh and blood reminders
of people who died under duress
from those whose duty is to protect.

>	July 19, 2015
>	Samuel DuBose, 43, Cincinnati, OH

>	August 7, 2015
>	Christian Taylor, 19, Arlington, TX

>	August 9, 2014
>	Michael Brown, 18, Ferguson, MO

They are flesh and blood reminders
of people who were killed
by those who will walk away.

CHAPTER 4

STAYING INSIDE

Oh, I don't go out anymore. I just stay inside. I keep my doors locked, except for when I let Millie in. Millie gets me what I need. She goes to the store for me, gets my mail so I can pay my bills, and runs other little errands I need done. I don't know what I'd do if I didn't have Millie. She's good to me. I don't have anybody else, not after Henry died. It cost me quite a bit to have Millie come three times a week, but I don't mind paying her. If I watch my pennies, Henry left me enough to get by. Having her come lets me live how I want to live now. There are so many horrible things going on these days. I just won't put myself in such danger. Anything can happen, like that time when I was at Kroger's, in the middle of the day mind you, and this man comes up from behind me when I was putting my groceries in the car, pushes me to the ground, and runs off with my purse. I think I was seventy-four or five at the time. Can you imagine anyone doing that to a lady that age?

It wasn't too long after that I had a run-in with another man. He was crazy. I'm sure of that. I was driving down the road, and I guess I wasn't being as careful as I should have been, and my car slid over into the lane next to mine, and I barely touched this other car. Well, I did what I should have. I pull over to the side of the road, and the car I kicked stopped too. This crazy man gets out his car and looks at his car. He starts cursing, saying the most vile things I've ever heard. Then he opens up his trunk and pulls out a baseball bat. He comes over to my car and starts beating my hood and my front lights. All the while he's yelling at me, telling me I should keep off the road, that I'm too old to be driving. Then he comes over to my window—I had already locked the car when he was carrying on the way he was—and he leans down, puts his big face right in front of mine, and says in the meanest way you can imagine, "Let this be a lesson to you. Stay off the road." He added the "B" word which I won't say. Then he stands up, walks back to his car, twirling his bat, like he's pleased with what he's done. He gets in and drives off. Well, I was just sitting there shaking. I could hardly breathe. I don't know how I managed to get myself home.

I don't leave the house now. As I said, Millie gets me what I need, and I enjoy her company. On the days she comes, we have lunch together. I miss going out, but I fill my time. I still do my own cleaning, except for the heavy stuff—Millie helps me with that. I look at my scrapbooks and remember all the good times Henry and I had. I watch my TV shows, but whenever the news comes on, I change the channel. I don't like to hear the things they talk about. The world has become a terrible place. It didn't use to be that way. People were nice to each other. You could count on their kindness. But now, there are so many people who are just mean, mean down to the bone. Staying inside, I keep my old bones safe.

CHAPTER 4

LAST WORDS

I always thought for your last meal you could get anything you wanted. But the reality is that you can get anything you want from that greasy spoon just down the road from the prison. Frank's Café is the name of it. I saw it when they were driving me here. An old beat-up place that stays in business just because it's so close to the prison. I ordered the only thing I thought might be good–cheeseburger and some fries. It wasn't very good or maybe I just wasn't much in the mood for eating. Knowing you only have hours left does something to your appetite.

I've spent a long time waiting for this day. I've come to accept it. Can't say I'm happy about it though. I rather have more time, even if I'm locked up in this shit hole. A bed. A toilet. That's all I got. I guess it's 12 X 12, but I don't know for sure. They don't provide a tape measure. When the time comes, they say I won't feel it, that they'll put me to sleep first, but I must admit I don't much trust what people tell you around here. They also say I'll have a chance for some last words. They'll be some people there. They'll be able see me, but I won't be able to see them. I could say that I am sorry I took the life of those people, and I regret the pain I've caused to their families and loved ones. But, to tell you the truth, I don't feel that way. I'd be lying if I said that. You see, when you kill people, you become numb to them. You don't think about who those people are, what their lives are, who might love them. They're just faces you need to put an "x" across. Cross them off the list. Get your money. That's how it works.

Now you're here, Father, asking me if I want to ask God for forgiveness. I'm not looking for forgiveness, not God's, not anybody's. I did what I did. I can't take that back, and if I was in the same situation, I'd probably do it again. They were nothing to me, and I needed the money. You see, it's simple: You reduce people to nothing, don't let yourself think about them, and it's easy. You just pull the trigger. Bang and it's over. You have a job, and you do it. It's that simple. If you let yourself start thinking, then it's harder. You just do it. You know the risks. Forgiveness is not part of the equation.

WHEN THOSE WE CALL GREAT FALL

When those we call great fall,
when the unwanted news claims
the screen, showing image
after same image, of their refusal
to comment, the covering hand
coming to the camera's eye,
when pundit after pundit pushes
on and on, filling every column inch
and broadcast minute, we sit
in dead silence, still as a
fallen branch, splintered,
the rot settling in.

When those we call great fall,
when they toss in their beds and turn
inward, when they tell themselves
that what they did was,
if not right, understandable,
when their tales trouble truth,
they climb out of bed and sit
in the dark, alone, shadowless,
taking stock, tallying their losses.
When their tears track their way
straight into their sorrows, they sink
into their self-serving lies.

When those we call great fall,
when they leave their locked houses,
accompanied by their partner's
dead stare, to publicly say
only what they think they must,
when they confess offering no

details or without telling why,
when they ask for God's guidance,
for forgiveness from all those
they've hurt, they pick their words
like lint from an old shirt, seeking
the same shape they once knew.

When those we call great fall,
their superiors and sycophants,
out of some sense of self-protection
or defense, struggle toward tales
to keep themselves in place. They,
caught between the hand that feeds
and the hand that burns, have
choices to make. They speak,
watching themselves, waiting to see
how the current accounts pull
them in, pull them here and there,
how they might wiggle until safe.

When those we call great fall,
when their hard-won honors
and awards are withdrawn,
when their plaques and statues
become nothing more
than a bird perch, they drop
from sight, hide from places
that once brought applause.
When they see the public facing
another's failure publicly plastered,
they pause, knowing how their
soft flesh sheds its skin.

When those we call great fall
we fall with them, their failures
finger their way into our hearts.

When their frailties figure
into our faith in the best of us,
we are frozen, frightened by
the math of more and less.
And when we flirt with forgiveness,
we find we are and are not
like them, that we will carry them,
that we will not forget their falls
and the sad fortunes of once.

CHAPTER 5

AGING, ILLNESS, AND DEATH LESSONS

THE WORRY LIST

The mere scratch that takes too long to heal, the hangnail that keeps screaming red, the sour breath right after a good brush.

The discolored blemishes that appear on the surprised skin; the parasitic dark moles that grow under the arms, on the back, around the neck; and the returning dry-skin sore that hides in the hair.

The ears that hardly hear, leaning in to gather as words fall to their grave.

The eyes, uneven in their power, that strain, that through their blur see parents who cannot see.

The fingers that curl, turn down into a claw, unable to form a tight fist, whose joints hold morning pain and the complaints of use, whose swollen knuckles keep the wedding band deep into place.

The feet that swell with the play and labor of the day, that find small comfort in the label plantar fasciitis, that seek elevation without any pressure on the heels.

The knees that wobble, that dread stairs, that bend with regret; the rounded shoulders that stiffen, straighten only with pain; and the back that only escapes discomfort by standing, by drugs.

The belly that protrudes, flops over the belt like an unwelcomed neighbor who hangs over a fence; the stomach that refuses to settle after being fed, that burps reminders, that flushes into the dark unknown.

CHAPTER 5

The breath that tries to catch itself after little more than a flight of stairs; the blood pressure that's too high, controlled by a small blue pill; the pulse that races right after a good night's sleep well over 100 beats per minute.

The heart, in its quiet ache, that wonders.

The years that keep time.

SURFACES

Knowing I work for the paper, my therapist suggested I do a story dealing with my fear of tiny surfaces, not about my phobia per se, but to find stories that would put me in contact with people whose work demands such daily encounters. I did a story on a professional chess master who moves pieces from one of those tiny squares to another, a report on a manicurist who paints nails in various designs. I even interviewed a seamstress whose thimble tapped pinhead after pinhead while we spoke. Believing I was cured, I started carrying coins again, quarters at first, but then pennies and dines. Ate lima beans, corn, even peas. I wore my mother's ring.

Then, he came to town, set up shop in the mall. He was my test. "How long have you been a rice artist?"

"Years," he answered. "My brother taught me. Said I needed to write 'Christopher' on a grain before I was ready to go out on my own."

His steady hand continued, his eyes focusing on his intricate task. I began to sweat.

"I also work with mustard seeds, a symbol of faith for Christians. I write 'Praise the Lord' on them."

I stiffened, became short of breath. I felt him take my hand. "Here," he offered, moving toward me with tweezers, holding my name on a single white grain. He dropped it in my palm. I closed my hand.

It's been a week now since he put it in there. I keep my fist tight, always closed. I feel myself sliding around, slipping, in there. I can't let go.

CHAPTER 5

WOMAN HOSPITALIZED

1.

Hot dust refusing
to settle, invisible,
in Winter's gray, still.

2.

Dark months
inside plastic
wrapped in tight, trapped,
canned by Chernobyl, afraid
of air.

3.

There once was a woman from Langeboom
Who only left her sofa to use the bathroom
From canned food she would eat
While wrapped in a plastic sheet
Because of the Chernobyl boom boom.

ON GOING NUTS

Going nuts means you no longer feel contained, wrapped up in a pretty bow, presentable to others. You are inappropriately leaking, perhaps behaving in ways that you shouldn't act, spewing words that you shouldn't say, or shedding tears that you shouldn't let escape.

You are breaking the rules and you want to stop, but you can't stop, can't stop the crazies. You are possessed. A strange force is taking control, taking you, or what you consider to be you, into its grasp.

You struggle to hang on. You try to gather verbs so that you know what you should do.

You want to fight it back, but you soon see that your efforts are pointless. You give yourself over, surrender to another you who you come to see as yourself. You do not like this other you. You wish it would leave, allow you to breathe with more ease. You want the comfort of your prior self, the one who can move around the world, perhaps not with confidence, but with some invisibility.

You want to be able to complete your day. You do not like being a spectacle, a disturbance, a patient that needs attending.

You do not find comfort in the various diagnostic labels you can apply to your other you. You would rather deny the existence of that you. To name it gives it presence. But there you are, trying on labels as if to see what clothes have the best fit.

You rather run down the street naked than be exposed like you are.

You see them watching you, the you you'd rather them not see. They look puzzled, concerned. They do not know what to say or do. You wish they would leave you alone. They try to connect with words that you can't hear, with touch that you can't feel.

CHAPTER 5

You want a place where nothing is happening.

You are living in the moment. The only future you desire is the one without the other you. The only past you want is a return, a handle on your more familiar you.

You are alone, frightened, as if your body has turned into a thousand mice who are scurrying away from a falling foot. Your life is that moment.

GOING HOME

I can't forget they are in their seventies.
I believe them more now than ever
when they say, "We can't do what we use to."

In my uneasy mind I have been waiting
for the call: We had to take your ...
The rest is too clear.

But now I drive to see their good health.
I am always shocked by age,
how time holds no secrets.

The walk is less steady, the face,
as they say, has more character.
They are of another era.

He flirts, she smiles.
She cooks, he eats.
He still works, she still buys.

They are, if not happy, content,
hoping to live out their days without
sickness, pity, or my poems.

CHAPTER 5

WHEN

When you become a parent to your mother and father, you worry whenever they are alone, afraid they'll forget to take their pills, afraid they'll become confused, afraid that their poor eyesight and hearing will put them in harm's way, afraid that their illnesses of the thyroid, of the pancreas, of the heart, and of the deteriorating brain will soon take control;

when the home you grew up in turns into a quiet place of long afternoon naps, of soft voices over hot tea, of bedroom slippers on carpet laid over hardwood floors, becomes a place for storage of photo albums and mementos from trips they can no longer take, of Christmas and birthday gifts you gave when you couldn't imagine what they might want, of fine china never used, of clothes too small or too big, and of outdated computers gathering dust; when the home you remember, which once seemed large enough for everyone, keeps getting smaller, with the upstairs and back room shut off and the car gone, with the garden over-grown, and with the fence ready to fall and the roof ready to leak, you begin to understand;

when you know more about their business than they do; when you write checks for them to sign, deal with confusing medical bills, disrupted services, and essential house care; when you ask about how they would like to handle this or that and they answer with "whatever you think best," but before they answer, you notice them freeze for just a moment as they realize that it's best for you to make decisions on their behalf, and they seem sad and tired, you recognize a bit more;

when you wonder if the grandchildren are too much for them to handle, even though they say they're not; when they prefer to stay home from events they never would have missed; when they name the friends they've lost, the ones you knew better than your aunts and uncles who are also gone; when you see how slowly they walk as they make their way to the bedroom after announcing that 9:00 is past their bedtime, you see everything more clearly;

when, without warning, a copy of their will arrives in the mail; when they start sentences with "I don't want to be a bother" and "After we're gone," and say with finality, "We've had a good life" and when you, trying to sound upbeat and to be comforting, say back, "You've got lots more years in you," even though everyone knows that probably isn't true, and your words hit their ears as a burden, then, and only then, do you recognize your use.

CHAPTER 5

THE END OF AN ACADEMIC CAREER

The body—my body—is losing life one letter at a time.
(Goodall, 2012, p. 725)

The pile of the past is larger than the pile of the future. I feel the tug, the pull to what was and what might be. I cling to the passing present, holding on, letting go, trying to discover which way to turn. Time, an incessant pulse, pushes on. It only looks ahead, regardless of what or who is left behind. There is no smashing it against a rock or stabbing its machinery with a screwdriver. It's all prefigured, set. The present is only a tick between the before and after. It is time for me to address this slow drag forward, this slipping away of what has been so meaningful to me. In this narrative autoethnography, I explore the desire to hang on and to let go as I find myself at a time in my life when the years I have left are significantly less than the years I've already lived. I proceed by offering fragmentary accounts, ones that stand as worry points in my own experience. Organized around my attempts to hang on and to let go of my academic career, I write, marking moments of tension in a life script, in the desire to demonstrate how predictable life changes do not come without consideration and cost.

    Each entry emerges as a momentary act of sense-making, a narrative that won't hold still. Following Goodall (2000), I strive for a dialogic engagement where readers might find points of identification and might see culture doing its thinly veiled work. I move forward in the spirit of Goodall's call:

> New ethnography is a cultural way of coding academic attempts to author a *self* within a *context of others*. It is a way of writing to get to the *truth* of *our* experiences. It is a method of inquiry, scholarly inquiry, that privileges the exploration of a self *in response to questions that can only be answered that way*, through the textual construction of, and thoughtful reflection about, the *lived experiences of that self.* (p. 191, italics in the original)

In this act of sharing my story, I carry Goodall's (2008) counsel: "The very act of writing a story... *alters the way we think about* what we know and how we know it" (p. 14, italics in the original). I write wanting to know. Goodall's words tell me how to proceed. He has been helping me move forward as a narrative autoethnographer for many years now, allowing me to walk in his shadow, offering words that model and inspire, outlining and displaying the power of qualitative inquiry. He encourages me to live in the communicative "mystery" of daily life and to work with the attentive eye of the detective puzzling through a case. He reminds me that my life, like all lives, is narratively constructed, built not only by the muscle of persuasive argument but, more importantly, by the relational dynamics stories enable. I let my tale unfold under his continuing influence.

HANGING ON

Except for the two years I spent participating in the Vietnam war, or as the Vietnamese prefer to call it, the American war (Nguyen, 2012), of my early years, I've been teaching in various universities since 1969. My longest academic tour of duty has been at Southern Illinois University. I've always found my greatest allegiance with the faculty in the trenches than with those who send missives from above. It's been the MOS (Military Occupation Specialty) of my choice. I've always enjoyed participating in battle plan conversations, searching for the pedagogical weapon that would make a difference. With them, I've celebrated large and small victories and lamented setbacks, casualties, and losses. I've read what they wrote, often took their words as marching orders. I've written to them, hoping I might have a place in their ranks, might hold a flag they would stand behind.

I cannot push this military metaphor any further, not without misrepresenting my own daily sense of engagement in higher education. I have never considered academic life as a battle with students, colleagues, or administrators, although at times I've felt embattled. I have never believed scholarly disagreements were intentional acts of critical killing, although at times I've felt as if I'd been attacked. I've never thought of hostile students as my enemy, although at times I've wanted to ban one or two from my classroom. Instead, the academy of my experience emerges as a series of never ending questions, conundrums, difficult and intricate, leading, at best, to tentative answers. Whatever I bring to the classroom and whatever I publish, I see as momentary hunches, as the best guess I can make in a given instant. The joy of academic life for me has always been that the puzzles I've tried to solve in the classroom and in my research never settle, never feel resolved, fixed. With each new class and research project, new questions emerge. With each completed class and research project, questions linger. What seduces, what gets me out of bed each morning, is the unattainable, the unreachable. No perfect class ever happens—it is only the desire to achieve such an end that keeps me going, that continues to fascinate and motivate. No book or scholarly essay ever provides the last word—it is only the wish to be the best conversational partner I can bring forth that drives me to the computer, that insists that I keep working, keep struggling to hold down what will always wiggle out of my grasp. And so, I hold on, wanting the challenges that never end, that I'll never master, that come to me as daily gifts.

LETTING GO

I no longer hear as well as I once did. Most voices come to my ears with ease; some slide by as a soft mumble. I hear myself saying in class, "Help an old deaf man. Would you mind repeating what you just said?" The students are generous and they comply with my request, but the next time they speak, they fall back into their normal speech patterns. I move toward them, trying to hear what they have to offer, trying to take their words in. When I can't, I wonder if I should ask again, ask for the accommodation, ask for their tolerance, and I wonder if I should just go away, decide my years are done, accept that I should no longer be there. I am becoming the photographer who cannot see, the ditch digger who cannot lift the shovel, the doctor who cannot find a stethoscope. I should let go.

HANGING ON

Like Hart (1993), I like teachers for how they "think," "feel," and "act" (pp. 98–100). Even when they marshal their keen intelligence for purposes in direct opposition to my own or when their arrogance chips away at their own wisdom, I like being around them, like being in their company. I must admit, though, that I like them least when they simply see their arguments as eloquent and logically sound articulations, safe from counter-arguments and critical dismissal and when they flex their academic muscles at others' expense. I like them best when they understand how their ideas are relational, connecting points between people, carrying consequences in people's lives. I like them best when they participate in ongoing academic talk as conversational partners, sensitive to other voices and confident that their words will never be the final authority. I like them best when they are vulnerable, unafraid to admit that they have not read everything they think they should, unafraid to acknowledge their own limitations, unafraid to say "I don't know." At their best, academics create a culture of the curious and the humble that trusts more in the "maybe" and the "perhaps" than in the certain.

Perhaps, that is why I cling to this culture, this academic way of being. I enjoy being a person who has a place in the conversation. It makes me the kind of person I want to be, reflexive, pushed to my capacities, privileged to be with scholars, thinking and feeling our way, demanding daily more and more of ourselves. I worry, as I consider walking away, that books and journals will sit on my desk gathering dust, that I will settle too easily for the night's offerings on television, that I will have nothing of worth to say. So, for now, I stay.

LETTING GO

Over a lovely dinner, Ronald Shields, a professor at Bowling Green State University and a man close to my age, remarked, "The time to get out is before they start calling you the stink at the end of the hall." I worry that I'm beginning to smell.

HOLDING ON

I find myself in an informal conversation with several graduate students outside our office building. It's a beautiful fall day. The squirrels are gathering nuts while the afternoon sun keeps our coats unzipped and our talk playful. One of the graduate students mentions that she has been invited to speak to our undergraduate Introduction to Communication Theory class on performance studies. "I want to talk about how the shift from oral interpretation to performance studies made the body central," she says. She pushes on describing the history she wants to share. Her history is history I have lived and I feel the need to offer my oral history to her account. "Old folks, like me, who worked under the label of oral interpretation thought the body was pretty central to what we were doing," I begin, trying my best not to dampen her excitement about giving her talk. She quickly sees what I'm doing and asks me to elaborate. I go on and on, offering more than she probably wanted, but I leave the conversation feeling I've been of use. I like feeling that way. I like seeing myself as more than junk, more than something to be discarded.

LETTING GO

It happened during a "talk-back" session following a graduate student directed show on the Kleinau stage. I was attempting to make a point that the production didn't allow sufficient entry for the audience, that it was difficult to see why the characters were seduced by what they were saying, that it was hard to imagine why someone would be pulled into the world created. The director gave a quick response: "This show was not for you." I do not know what the director intended by those words, but I heard the remark as a comment on my age, that I was too out-of-touch with a topic from a generation that came later than my own, that I was calling forward aesthetic standards from a previous time. I heard the comment as a dismissal, as someone saying I no longer needed to be heard.

HOLDING ON

"Your father was so happy after he retired," my mother says, trying to encourage me to enjoy life without work. I see him sitting in his chair, taking the day to read the morning paper. He sits, waiting for a visit from his children or grandchildren. He sits, watching television and swallowing his pills. He sits, trying to remember details from his life. He sits, his shoes still in his closet. I am not ready to sit.

LETTING GO

I think of Laurel Richardson, retired, still presenting conference paper after conference paper, writing book after book. She offers a script, a way of being that has some appeal. I can see myself living as if I were on an extended sabbatical, writing each day, free from administrative and teaching responsibilities, free just to write. But if I'm living outside the academic community, I wonder if the isolation will pull me into whirlpool of doubt: Why am I doing this? Does anyone care? Should I still be taking journal space? Does it matter that I would no longer need to turn in my vitae at the end of the year? Would the hard work of making words come together on the page feel like speaking in an empty room? Outside the community, would I continue to believe that research matters? Would I begin to accept that my writing was just a strategy for getting an academic pat on the back? Was it all just about my ego?

HOLDING ON

I ask my graduate assistant to find some research on life span research. I tell her I want to look at what the research says about people my age. Certain that my struggles with retirement are no more than a cliché, I want to cite some material that would demonstrate what I think I already know. She returns with several books on aging (Harwood, 2007; Hummert & Nussbaum, 2001; Tepper & Cassidy, 2004). I glance through the table of contents: medical care and health facilities, disorders of old age, preventing elder abuse, family caregiving, enhancing communication with older adults, stereotypes about aging, and the uses of media. I put the books aside, denying what I most likely will have to face. That's not me, not yet, not now. When I do find the research (e.g., Adams & Beehr, 2003; Pinquart & Schindler, 2007; Sheehy, 1974, 2006; Taylor & Shore, 1993) I want, I confirm my suspicion: I am a cliché.

CHAPTER 5

My graduate assistant also returns with an article entitled, "Faculty Development in Speech Communication: Issues Surrounding the Retirement Phase." In this piece, Auer (1983) argues that institutions should do a better job helping retired faculty to see that they can still be of use, that they do not fall into the belief "that retirement marks the end of growth, is a slowing up, and a termination of self-actualization" (p. 26). His solutions (e.g., access to library services, permanent parking privileges and faculty club membership, free mailing and supplies for university business, continuation of graduate student advisement, participation in graduation ceremonies) might appeal to me when I walk away, but I leave Auer's essay feeling patronized, convinced that leaving is walking away from what satisfies.

LETTING GO

I have dinner with a dear friend from my graduate school days at a national convention. For the last several years she had been struggling with whether or not to retire; we would sit together talking, an urgency in her questions of what could be next for us, of what life outside the academy might mean. Now, she seems at peace with her decision to leave. I sense a new calm in her, a readiness, an excitement about the next phrase of her life. "I plan to give full attention to my creative writing," she says. "I have several plays that I want to work on." She has authored an unwritten retirement script, a script that serves as a guide to the future. I envy her and wonder if the urgency in my own body will subside once I settle into a new way of being, a script that tells me what to do next. Like my friend, I can see myself writing, turning to poetry, playing with words day after day, until something I might call a poem emerges. I can see myself writing in the morning and playing golf in the afternoon, still trying to move that silly ball around, even if it is from the front tees. I can see myself reading novels, ones I've wanted to read but had difficulty finding the time to put into my schedule. I can see myself living in a warm climate, even though thoughts of moving seem overwhelming. Perhaps, I can see a future.

HOLDING ON

During a break from the college promotion and tenure committee, I find myself talking with a senior faculty member from the creative writing program at SIU. Our conversation falls into the subject of retirement and I share a fantasy I've had: "I was thinking it might be fun to return to school to get a MFA in creative writing," I say. My comment seems to send her into distant thought and she remarks, as if wondering out loud, "Well, we have had some older people in the program. Once we admitted a man in his forties." I am thrown instantly into an image of myself, sitting at the end of a table of twenty-somethings, each with their poems spread out, each wondering if they will have to waste their time listening to an old man. I feel a future script fall away, fall like a loose brick from a crumbling building.

LETTING GO

I spend several days of Thanksgiving break reading an advisee's doctoral dissertation. It is good work, a document that the student should take proudly to the table. As I move through the pages, though, I find myself nodding off, not because of the quality of the work, but because I don't want to be reading another dissertation, another document that I must mark, that I must judge. I feel the weight of the critical enterprise, the never-ending assessment. Goodall's (2000) assertion, "academic life is a life of *constant* criticism" (p. 25, italics in the original), reminds me how the critical life produces a culture of broken bones.

HOLDING ON

Friends enrich life, providing substance and support, and mine all reside in the academy. A dear friend who teaches at another university says, "If you retire, when will I ever see you." Our relationship has been maintained by finding time together at conventions, time I've cherished, time I don't want to lose. But once conventions no longer figure into my new life routines, once that time evaporates, we will drift apart, each in life patterns that do not cross. When I retire, I may have

CHAPTER 5

an occasional lunch with departmental friends, but the glue of those relationships—departmental business, students we share, university life—will turn daily interactions into empty shells. I will no longer be a stakeholder in what matters most to them. I will become the person who once was a part of it all, a historical relic tolerated at the annual Christmas lunch, a reminder of what they rather not face.

LETTING GO

Nassbaum and Baringer (2000) note, "Three aspects of the cognitive system—working memory, processing speed, and name retrieval—appear to exhibit age-related change and to have an effect on language processing and production capabilities of older adults" (p. 204). I am standing in a graduate seminar when a student makes an excellent point. It triggers in my mind a book that I think she would enjoy. "There is this book you would like," I say with excitement. I pause, trying to pull up the title and author. "It has a blue cover. Wait. It will come to me. It's on my third shelf in my office. I think it's my third shelf. I know it will come to me. It really is worth your time. Sorry, I just can't bring it forward. If you follow back to my office after class, I'll let you borrow it." After class, I find it on my second shelf. I use to pride myself on how I could name references in class, often giving date of publication and publisher, how I could point to the source I wanted to remember as well as to other related pieces. Now, remembering names and titles is like trying to hold air. Students deserve better.

HOLDING ON

I usually arrive at the office a bit before 8:00. I unpack my bag and turn on the computer. My first morning tasks are to see what email must be answered and to prepare for classes. Throughout the day I handle administrative duties, talk with students, teach my classes, go to lunch with colleagues, find short periods to write a few words, chit-chat by the faculty mail boxes, attend meetings, and so on. I embrace, needless to say, some of these activities with more enthusiasm than others. I know the texture of this daily life; this typical faculty routine is settled into my being. It's a routine so familiar that it comes to me without reflection—it is just what I do. Whenever the question—what would you do if you won the lottery? —would arise, I always would have the same answer: I would keep doing what I'm doing. I enjoy my routine, believe it is worth doing, find comfort in knowing what each task entails.

LETTING GO

Many years ago every member of our department moved from electric typewriters to computers, except the chair who was still working on a manual typewriter. It was a clear sign that his days as chair were limited. I do not move around the web with the same facility as my colleagues. I do not know the full capabilities of my computer. I hang on to my Windows XP operating system. I have little use for a smart classroom. I've never taught a class using power point. I resist on-line teaching and the use of Blackboard. I do not have a Twitter account and seldom check Facebook. My days are limited.

HOLDING ON

"It's such a male thing," a female colleague says, "letting your identity be tied to your profession." And she is right: my sense of self is knotted to my job, perhaps more so because I am a man. In a culture that establishes men primarily as laborers and that measures worth by productivity, I am called forth as a small bit in the cultural economic machine. This is what men do. They work and good men give a good day's work for a day's wages. Guilty of being trapped by this cultural logic, I move forward unable to shake what I have been taught. No matter that once your use comes to an end you are tossed aside. Someone will easily and eagerly replace you. Some younger body is always there, ready to step in, ready to keep culture going. I do not want to be replaced. Not just yet. Who would I be?

LETTING GO

She is ready, my wife for over thirty years, ready to put her academic career behind her, ready for a warmer climate, ready to leave our small town for the energy of a larger city. She has been waiting for me, waiting for a breath of different air. "I think I can handle one more year," she says, "if you're really not ready." I want to make her happy.

HOLDING ON

It's a failure of the imagination, a failure to envision a future that might please, a failure to see happiness beyond the academy. I would like to be the kind of person who counts with eager anticipation the months and days until the office door can finally be shut and who relishes with deep peace how time will be spent. I would like to be the kind of person who cheerfully purges his or her office of files, wall decorations, supplies, dissertations, books, and memorabilia. I would like to be the kind of person who walks away without regret and fear. I am not that person, not now.

LETTING GO AND HOLDING ON

Time will tell; it always does. I end without resolution, without a firm narrative to guide my way. The truth of my experience leads to several uncertain truths: perhaps, I am a sad figure, a pathetic cliché who refuses to accept the inevitable. It's time to just move on, to get out of the way. Perhaps, I've given myself enough reasons to stay, to keep doing what satisfies, at least for a few more years. Perhaps, I've shared a culturally loaded story, a typical conundrum in a life script, a difficult and complicated moment that many face with more or less effort and grace, and, in doing so, may allow others to see how thoughts about retirement might unfold, might feel. Perhaps, I've made a case for time's power, as if time needed someone to speak on its behalf, as if time cares. Perhaps, I've gained a better sense of why this decision has been so problematic for me, why I am so wedded to the connection between self-worth and work, why I feel "the body—my body—is losing life one letter at a time" (Goodall, 2012, p. 725).

I think of Bud Goodall, working to the very end. I reach for another cigarette, take a puff, and wonder what's next.

REFERENCES

Adams, G. A., & Beehr, T. A. (Eds.). (2003). *Retirement: Reasons, processes, and results.* New York, NY: Springer.
Auer, J. J. (1983). Faculty development in speech communication: Issues surrounding the retirement phase. *Association for Communication Administration Bulletin, 42,* 24–27.
Goodall, H. L., Jr. (2000). *Writing the new ethnography.* Lanham, MD: AltaMira.
Goodall, H. L., Jr. (2008). *Writing qualitative inquiry: Self, stories, and academic life.* Walnut Creek, CA: Left Coast Press.
Goodall, H. L., Jr. (2012). Three cancer poems. *Qualitative Inquiry, 18,* 724–727.
Hart, R. (1993). Why communication? Why education? Toward a politics of teaching. *Communication Education, 42,* 97–105.
Harwood, J. (2007). *Understanding communication and aging: Developing knowledge and awareness.* Los Angeles, CA: Sage.
Hummert, M. L., & Nussbaum, J. F. (Eds.). (2001). *Aging, communication, and health: Linking research and practice for successful aging.* Mahwah, NJ: Lawrence Erlbaum.
Nassbaum, J. F., & Baringer, D. K. (2000). Message production across the life span: Communication and aging. *Communication Theory, 10,* 200–209.
Nguyen, Q. H. (2012, May). *Performance methodology of memory work with Vietnamese Americans.* Paper presented at the Eighth International Congress of Qualitative Inquiry, Urbana-Champaign, IL.
Pinquart, M., & Schindler, I. (2006). Changes in life satisfaction in the transition to retirement: A latent-class approach. *Psychology and Aging, 22,* 442–455.
Sheehy, G. (1974, 2006). *Passages: Predictable crises of adult life.* New York, NY: Ballantine.
Taylor, M. A., & Shore, L. M. (1995). Predictors of planned retirement age: An application of Beehr's model. *Psychology and Aging, 10,* 76–83.
Tepper, L. M., & Cassidy, T. M. (Eds.). (2004). *Multidisciplinary perspectives on aging.* New York, NY: Springer.

CHAPTER 5

STILL WAITING

For those of us who are still waiting
for her ninety-six years to find their end,
who gather under her name, Mom,
who know this time there will be no
bouncing back, that cancer will assert
its will, who wake in the dark, sweating,
wondering if perhaps she's passed,
who do and do not want to be
by her side, to hold her dry hands,
to chat about nothing without ever
mentioning why we are sitting there,
who hold our breath when we see signs,
it is as if the moon will never find
its way from behind these cloudy nights.

HOW TO WATCH YOUR MOTHER DIE

Don't sit there wanting to be anywhere else.
Don't make excuses to be with the others waiting outside her room.
Don't chat with others about how their lives have been.
Don't exchange worried glances with the nurses.
Don't rattle on and on about everything except her condition.
Don't claim a little food will make her feel better.
Don't feel relief when a doctor enters the room.
Don't watch the doctor's every move.
Don't allow yourself to believe you might get a different prognosis.
Don't say she's doing about the same when others ask.
Don't keep fixing her bed unless it needs fixing.
Don't stop holding her hand.
Don't check your phone, again and again.
Don't complain that your back hurts from sitting too long in a hard chair.
Don't use tissues to wipe away the bile.
Don't say the medicine will take the pain away.
Don't stare at her IV.
Don't tell her she will be fine.
Don't incessantly watch her monitors.
Don't pray if you are a person who never prays.
Don't assume you will be sitting there again tomorrow.
Don't believe that once she is unconscious you shouldn't say, "I love you."
Don't leave her room until she is gone.
Don't do what I did.

CHAPTER 5

OLD BONES

I'm ready to take my old bones to the woods, to sit dead still, and to let my flesh rot off. I can become food for those who have the energy to scavenge, for the worms to work their way, for some archeologist several centuries from now to thrill with the first sight of bone, white in the dark earth, only to lament on further inspection, that it belongs to yet another human long forgot.

It is good to have some value, to be someone worthy of the space it takes to feed, clothe, and shelter, but it would hardly matter if one more ant in the line, filled with self-import and determined purpose, would fall prey to some experimenting thumb.

But, of course, that would never be your thumb, your final solution. Instead, dear reader, you might separate yourself from this pathetic speaker, old deluded fool that he is; or you might continue your reading, believing it might help, just as Sartre and Camus continued, in their sad conundrum, to write their way out; or you might wish, as I do, to take, without question, your brittle bones to the welcoming woods. Together, we can feast on each other until we die.

CREMATION ENDINGS

1.

When I die, I want to be cremated, my ashes divided among my three children. Every day following the services, each child is to take just a pinch of my ashes to throw into wind. When all my ashes are gone, it will time for them to stop grieving, time for them to let go of their mother.

2.

Dad is in the garage. I couldn't handle having him in the house any longer. It felt wrong having him on the mantle. It was creepy. So he's in the garage now. I try not to think about it, but I can't help myself. I keep hearing him say, "I want to come inside. Please let me in."

3.

When we do a cremation, we just put them in there. Burns them right up. Takes two or three hours for the whole process to be done. Depends on their size. The little ones go quick. It gets pretty routine. If we have to hand over the ashes, we just put them in box. But, sometimes, we not really sure whose ashes are whose. Ashes are ashes. They never know the difference.

4.

Mom wanted her ashes to be scattered in the Grand Canyon so my brother and I drove for three days to honor her wish. We found a spot that we thought Mom would like. I said a few words and turned the urn upside down thinking the wind would catch her ashes and would gently float them down to the canyon bottom. But most of her just fell around my feet. I couldn't make myself pick her up or shove her over the side with my foot, so we just left her there, there on the edge.

CHAPTER 5

5.

I'm never happy when they want to cremate the body, particularly if they elect to go without a casket. I make a lot more money if I can sell them an eternal resting place with all the special comforts. There's good money in the casket business. You let the family think the deceased is buried in the casket, but that doesn't make good economic sense. As soon as the services are done, you dump that body and you do a little refurbishing and it's ready for the next one. That's how you really make a good profit.

6.

It's the bones that don't fully turn to ash. They turn to fragments. Bits and pieces. It's hard to make everything unrecognizable, gone for good. It's hard to erase a human life.

MORGUE

With the drunk drivers, the suicides, and the drugs
on New Year's Eve we get more than usual,
but we always follow procedures—log them in,
do the prep work, and put them to bed.
I've been here for seven years. Frank twelve.
We've seen how death settles in, makes its claim,
takes them away. It's not like in those movies
where bodies pop up or zombies, eyes
staring straight ahead, come at you.
That's just stupid. The job is really routine.
We're in the shipping business—
we take them in and ship them out.
Don't get me wrong. We're respectful.
After time though one is just like another—
some may be heftier or messier than others
but they're the same. Cold. Heavy. Eyes
glazed. Almost startled. She was like that
when we were rolling her back to the fridge.
Then the sheet moved and we just froze.
We both saw it at the same time. We watched
for another moment and again it moved.
She was breathing but she still had that look
like she belonged here, like she was ready
to let herself be empty space, eager
to swallow death's heart whole.

CHAPTER 5

BIEN

One-hundred-fifteen years
I carried my name,
Santiago Lazaro Perez,
gave it to a good wife
who now sits near
our dear Lady of Guadalupe
and to nine children, all
but two who I had to bury.
No está bien.

Now, I worked my patch
of banana, citrus, and mango,
worked every day of my life.
So bent
I could hardly pick.
Had to use my cane to reach
what I could not.
And each day I'd lug
with each full crate
the pain of an old body.
No está bien.

So, I took the ladder
I climbed so many times
to the orange grove,
set it against the nearest tree,
went up, tied a rope,
and pushed the ladder away.
My weight on my neck
pulled me straight again.
I swung, proud.
Está bien.

STILL THERE

When death comes
the body sinks
deep into bedding
deep into down.
The mouth opens
dry, dark as
an abandoned cave
silent, without.
The closed hands
drop their fingers.
The eyes forget
to look.
Nothing moves except
those who are
still there.

CHAPTER 5

RITUAL

Services are over—
my tie loose, your shoes off.
We sit just holding hands,
talking with relatives.

Our faces hold old smiles,
heads nod to retold tales,
and as we eat and drink,
hours curl like a spring.

Tomorrow we can grieve
in this motherless house.
We will search for tasks
that busy hands and feet

And in our coffin minds
we will call out in the quiet.

PASSING

Old Chautauqua Road shoots
straight down
from the town's only hill
inviting a speedy escape.

The twenty-year-old Bowman boy
took that path, and, perhaps,
to miss a deer or
to reach for another beer, lost

control. Even now, four years later,
a memorial, kept fresh with flowers,
marks the spot where the oak
carries his cross. Horizontally,

his name, Chris, is printed
eye-level for all who pass.

CHAPTER 5

THE GRAVE

She stands silently at the family farm grave,
sees herself staring at the freshly dug dirt
She is like him, outside herself, double
dead, alive as the breeze that fluffs her white shirt.

Held by his presence, she falls to her knees,
squeezes the burial mud in her smooth hands,
then wipes her face with all of him she knows.
I could be there to help her, but I'm not.

Instead, I stand in the shade of the tree, unsteady.
Afraid of the dead and dying, I turn away, anxious
to deny the future of what is too easy to name, ready
to put aside the thoughts of my own double selves.

ALWAYS BECOMING

You found yourself simultaneously growing larger and falling apart, slowly at first, but then you seemed to pick up momentum. Your body, more and more, gave you pause. You started noticing your changes by the accumulation of physical activities you once did with such ease that became harder and harder for you. You were less likely to participate in a full-court basketball game—half-court seemed plenty. You were less likely to select the four-mile trail over the two-mile trail, even though you knew the four-mile trail was much more picturesque. You were less likely to play more than eighteen holes of golf on a given day when in earlier times you would have been quick to squeeze in another nine holes. You were less likely to take the stairs if you saw an elevator nearby. You were less likely to take on chores; instead, you hired someone else to get them done. As you backed away from your more active habits, you considered such changes as a natural part of aging. You continued to eat too much, and it wasn't long before you were exercising too little.

You noticed that with each decade, you gained ten pounds. A pound a year didn't cause alarm; it didn't seem like much. But over time, the pounds added up. When you graduated college, you had a 32 inch waist; now you were squeezing into 38 inch pants. You never worried about what you were putting into your body and you had a particular fondness for anything that might be fried. At Christmas time, you and your brother would compare your widening girths. "I've got you beat again this year," you'd say, tapping your protruding stomach. During your enlarging period, your wife asked you if you'd like to walk around the neighborhood. You enjoyed those evening strolls, although you doubted if your moseys would improve your physical condition. One evening while walking you were engaged in conversation and you found yourself walking several miles. Plantar fasciitis struck the next day and your walking days ended for a couple of years. Your body collected additional pounds.

At a visit to the doctor's office in the hopes of scoring antibiotics for a sinus infection, you encountered a no-nonsense nurse. After weighing you and taking your blood pressure, she blurted out, "You need to lose some weight. If you don't, two things are in your future––a stroke and a nursing home." You were surprised by her bluntness, but the doctor said nothing and you let it pass after joking about it with your friends. It wasn't until you were dropping your daughter off for her first year of college and you stumbled across a free blood pressure machine did you take notice. According to the chart on the machine, your numbers, 190 over 100, were well beyond normal, stage two hypertension to be exact. The nurse's words came back to you and you decided you would check with your doctor. That's when you began taking a pill a day for your blood pressure.

    You still found yourself eating too many things you shouldn't, and you knew you were also eating too much. While on occasion you might notice an article on nutrition, you would never bother to read it. You watched yourself gain more pounds at the same time as your body kept finding more and more foods that gave you indigestion. Nothing seemed better than a large bowl of ice cream to soothe your rebellious stomach. If that didn't work, you always had Tums handy. You began to eye your wife's Prilosec.

    As your pounds increased, you witnessed a decrease in your senses. Your taste buds didn't seem as sensitive as they once were. Perhaps it was because you could not smell as well as you once did. Taste and smell, you read or heard somewhere, are connected. You blamed your troublesome sinuses for not being able to smell well. You tried nasal sprays, but none worked to open your sinuses. You accepted this, given where you were living. Besides, you thought, a loss of smell is fine when it's time to change the litter.

    Your sense of touch remained stable. You could still tell if something was hot or cold, rough or smooth, sticky or slippery. But you discovered it was harder and harder to close your fingers into a fist. Occasionally, one of your knees would give and you'd almost fall. Your neck was often stiff. Arthritis had set in, particularly bothersome after a round of golf or working in the yard. Aspirin became your friend.

    Your sight, particularly out of your right eye, was blurry. You had trouble driving at night, but you managed to pass your driver's renewal test every five years so you thought your seeing was sufficient. You liked not wearing glasses. Eventually, your wife convinced you to have your eyes checked: Cataracts in both eyes, one eye requiring immediate surgery, the other to follow. Now you need glasses to read, and your world remains as blurry as it was before surgery. You are grateful, though, that you did not lose your sight. You like being able to see. You remember that your ophthalmologist also mentioned that early signs of glaucoma were also present.

Your ability to hear, following in your parent's pattern, has had a slow and profound drop. You hear some voices better than others, but you are embarrassed by the frequency you have to repeat, "What did you say?" You have trouble hearing at work, and your wife will soon be wearing ears plugs when you want to watch television. Confounding matters, your ears, usually starting around mid-morning and lasting until late afternoon, feel stopped up, as if you just got off a plane. You went to your doctor who had no cure. He sent you to a specialist who had no cure. For two years you tried various drugs, too many to list, with no effect. You take your daily Zyrtec, but doubt if it does any good. You keep saying you want to get hearing aids, but you've been slow to act, remembering your parent's complaints about theirs and your doctor's recommendation to wait until your ears clear before investing. You live with the hearing you have.

As the power of your senses decreased, you needed oral surgery to pull a tooth that could no longer be repaired. You believe more teeth are soon to go. You called upon a dermatologist to remove the plague of moles growing in exponential numbers from your head to your feet. You now have fewer moles but more scars. Your wrinkled skin hangs on your bones. Your ankles swell if you stand or walk too long. Your back is in constant pain. You do daily exercises to build back strength, but that only seems to make matters worse. You keep your Biofreeze handy.

Despite it all, you consider yourself, given your age, lucky. No major diseases have come your way. No major injuries have struck. No major surgeries have been required. You keep chugging along, hoping for the best, but you know it is just a matter of time. You try to be philosophical about it all. What happens will happen, you say. In general, you try not to think about your health, not to let it slow you down. You sense, with some sadness, that it's more present for you than it has ever been. You are becoming, always falling away, falling into your own diminishment, falling into your last days. You are always becoming, closer and closer to the end.

CHAPTER 6

TELLING TRUTHS

AMERICAN BEAUTY

You would think they'd get it right. All the details they worried about—the cut of our suits, the color on our cheeks, the swing in our walks. The chaperones, with their straight backs and steady eyes, were always there. But when they gave their second announcement, I had to stand there, give that little hug, watch her walk down the walk-way swinging those hips, waving to everyone, with the crown shining as big as life, knowing it should have been me.

Now, I smile on all occasions, the Jill who is ready for every Jack that comes my way, ready for the moment, dressed and all, ready as candy for each boy with swimsuit dreams. So, when they rushed on stage to say the wrong girl was named, that surely I'd understand as they took my crown, this beauty queen saw her broadcast face, a snarl filling the large screen.

CHAPTER 6

KEN DOLL TURNS FORTY

Do tell, Mattel,
has his hair gotten a little thin,
has his belly begun to sag,
has his step slowed just a bit?

And does Barbara Millicent Roberts
still plan to marry Ken Carson?
Is Ken still the dream of Barbie's eye?
What's the scoop? Please tell.

And does Ken, now facing mid-life and
seeing his forty-two year old Barbie,
ever wonder how it might have been if
Barbie hadn't put her careers first,
or if he had decided to be with Midge,
or if, instead of smooth plastic, he had
a penis as big as Barbie's car?

PLAYING THE GAME

I'll tell them anything they want to get what I want. If they need me to say they're pretty, that's what I'll say. If they like to think of themselves as smart, I'll tell how impressed I am with how they put things together. And if they're worried about their weight, I'll tell them, no matter what their size is, that it's just what I like. It's how you play the game. The smart ones know you're gaming them, but if you do it with some skill, they'll go along because they appreciate how you put it out there. It's the dumb ones I sometimes feel bad about. It's like they thought something real was going on and then they get this look on their face when they realize what happened. I hate that look. It's like they've been broken a bit. You know, kind of a sad and hurt look, their hair falling around their face, and their eyes filling up. And they don't stand quite as straight as they were before. But that's part of it. A man has got to do what a man has got to do.

There was this one woman though—beautiful, just the shape I like, and smart too. Too smart. She got me good. I met her at The Shadow, that dance bar not far from here. You know the one. I saw her dancing, showing off her moves. She was hot, had everybody watching her. Well, I got some moves of my own, so I made my move, and before you know it, we were dancing and I was buying her drinks. Right before I was going to ask her if she wanted to get out of there for some alone time between just the two of us, she says she has to leave, but that she wants to see me again real soon. She leans her body into mine as she says this and runs a couple fingers down my face. Her message was clear. A couple nights later, I see her again and basically the same thing happens. Only this time before she leaves, she gives me this long kiss and lets her hand rub up against my stuff. I have to admit she had me. I wanted her bad. About a week later, I see her again, and after we have a few drinks, she asks me if I want to come back to her place. Like I said, I was ready, so I follow her in my car to this big apartment building. We get to the front entrance and three guys grab me before I know what happened. They take me out back, beat the shit out of me, and take my phone, my wallet, and my car. They left me there with nothing. It was all a set up. She took me in good.

CHAPTER 6

She had me believing that she was as hot for me as I was for her. The cops found my car a couple of days later; it was stripped—no wheels, no battery, nothing, not even the front seats. They never got the guys who punched, kicked, and robbed my sorry ass. I tried to find her, but I never saw her again. She knew what she was doing. She lied to me every inch of the way. I can't believe I fell for it, but I did. I still do my thing, but it's not fun like it used to be. I guess she took my fun, along with all my stuff. I guess you could say that she broke me.

THE LIES COUPLES KEEP

Partner 1:   Does this look okay on me?
Partner 2:   Yeah. You look great.

Partner 1:   Would you mind doing that touch up paint before my family comes on Friday?
Partner 2:   Not at all. I'll get it done.

Partner 1:   I cooked the meat a bit too long.
Partner 2:   I think it's fine.

Partner 1:   Does it bother you when I interrupt your work?
Partner 2:   No. I usually can use a little break.

Partner 1:   Do you have time to help me with this?
Partner 2:   Sure. What do you need?

Partner 1:   I've been practicing my scales quite a bit. Am I driving you crazy?
Partner 2:   No. I like hearing you play.

Partner 1:   I've made plans with our neighbors for Friday night. Is that okay?
Partner 2:   Great. It'll be fun.

Partner 1:   Was I in your way?
Partner 2:   No. I think I was in your way.

Partner 1:   I haven't paid the mortgage bill yet.
Partner 2:   Don't worry. It will get there before the due date.

Partner 1:   Do you like my old friend from college?
Partner 2:   Yeah. He seems real nice.

CHAPTER 6

Partner 1: I picked this out for your mother's birthday.
Partner 2: Mom will love it.

Partner 1: Did you throw away those shorts I love?
Partner 2: I wouldn't do that.

Partner 1: Does it bother you that I keep my desk so messy?
Partner 2: No. That's up to you.

Partner 1: You're late.
Partner 2: Really? I must have lost track of the time.

Partner 1: Did you put gas in the car?
Partner 2: Sorry. I forgot.

Partner 1: I know we just lost Sunshine, but I want another dog. Okay?
Partner 2: Sure, if that's what you want.

Partner 1: Did you look at my phone?
Partner 2: No. I wouldn't do that.

Partner 1: Do you know what caused this spot on the rug?
Partner 2: I have no idea.

Partner 1: Do you think I should have this mole under my eye removed?
Partner 2: That's up to you.

Partner 1: I love you.
Partner 2: And I love you.

NAILED DOWN

I don't like being nailed down. You never know when someone is going to hold what you said against you. So I always try to be vague, keep some wiggle room in what I'm saying. Ambiguity is my friend. Qualifiers, most of the time, cling to what I'm saying. I figure you can't be too careful, can't let them know where you stand. That way you can always deny what someone might accuse you of. The phrase, "I didn't say that," if you've prepared the proper groundwork, can be a happy companion. You'll never be caught in a lie.

You might be thinking that what I'm saying now is pretty concrete. Given what I've said, you might believe that I like to deceive people, that I'm not honest with them. But notice, I didn't say that. I never said that I lie, never said that I'm dishonest. I'm just careful so that I can't lie. I try to make sure that there is a truth in what I'm saying. See, I always want to tell the truth, but that's hard. This way I never lie and you never know if I am or not.

CHAPTER 6

ON THE STREETS

Not caring if they're heard,
they face each other.
We pretend not to listen.
We are not their audience.
We are not there.

His body jerks with each word—
spasms punctuating sounds
gestures striking the notes
of a jazz gone mad.
He wants her to change.

Her words drool,
slide out like worms.
"I'm only an old wino,"
she says again and again,
grabbing for his resisting arm.

We move beyond hearing
to an evening of theatre.

NEIGHBOR

Shuffling in house shoes and robe
to put the weekly garbage out,
I'm greeted by my neighbor:
"Hello there," he calls,
"Beautiful morning, isn't it?"
I answer with a strained,
"Yes," as I carry my old can, bottom
ready to go, beneath my belly.
I waddle down the drive and drop my load.
He is ready for the day, dressed
in the perfect coat and tie.
In one hand, he holds, carefully
away from his body, a single
bag of trash, tied tightly and
clean as his pressed white shirt.
In the other, a thin cardboard container
inscribed with bold bright letters,
"Ab Shaper," over an image of a
smiling perfect body that I swear
could be his own. Looking down, I see
on the top of my pile, precariously
perched, my large stuffed box
marked: "Deluxe Cheese Tray."

CHAPTER 6

THE TEACHER

Sitting at my desk while they nosily work, I wonder if they labor for themselves or for me, the man in power who has said this must be done. I've told them I'm here if they have any questions. No questions come my way as I just gaze out at the students.

I decide to stroll among the groups of three. As I approach, silence claims the space and eyes turn toward me. "Any problems?" They shake their heads implying that they can't understand why I intruded. When I arrive at the fourth group, a student has been anticipating my arrival: "Is this all we are going to do today? I don't find this a good use of my time."

I look at him and smile as I decide how best to respond. His two group members freeze, ready to turn whatever I will say into a story. I consider, "Well, I wouldn't want this class to interfere with your little life so please go do what you what you need to do." I settle on a less sarcastic reply: "I'm sorry you're not finding this task worth your time. See how you can make the best of it."

The student looks down, perhaps believing he may have said too much. I move on to the next group that has no questions, but he stays with me. A large part of me thinks he is right. He could be using his time more productively than completing my assignment. I wonder if I should tell the students that my purpose was to teach them that time is valuable and that only one student earned an "A."

BORDER CROSSING

1.

Going south you see the signs—
a faceless family of three,
a father, mother and child
fleeing across the highway,
mother clasping the child's wrist
as the father leads the way.
"CAUTION" the sign clamors
above the dark family figures
so the California motorists
won't trouble their day by
an accidental road kill.

2.

Build the fences higher.
Arrest them 'til they tire.

Call the border patrol.
We must keep control.

Hire more guards.
They're coming in our yards.

Shine your lights tonight.
We must protect our rights.

Build the fences higher.

3.

Crossing over, you wait
to be examined. Innocent
as skin you slide right through,
passing under their poison eyes.

CHAPTER 6

4.

Look at the line.
Tell me what's fair.
Look at the line,
then list what's mine.

Look at that child
peeking through the fence,
and tell me, por favor,
how a line makes sense.

5.

Watched by the guards,
they pass dollars
at Border Park
through an old fence
before it runs into the Pacific,
driven solid into the sand,
out just far enough to tempt,
but too far for success.
It is an engineering feat.

HELEN

They shouldn't have let so many of them in there. When I told them I'd do my act—Bob and his Amazing Bear Helen—and I'd do it for less than my usual cost since it was for the old folks, I had no idea how small the space would be. They just kept coming, shuffling in, one after another, leading with their canes, their walkers and their wheelchairs. I'm surprised that the home would let them do that. I bet it was against fire code. I didn't think my show would have such appeal. Usually I work birthday parties, some weddings. I guess they didn't have much else to do.

My act is simple. I got Helen after my wife of twenty-three years died of cancer. That was just two years ago. Named Helen after my wife. She just knows a few tricks. I try to make the best of them, stretch the program out. I tell some jokes, and Helen and I do a little dance together. I dress her up and we stroll around. She's something to see in her hat and all. In the big finale, she balances on a ball, goes forward and backward, first on all fours, and then, standing.

That's when it happened. I've trained Helen to always take five steps when going back. There was room if that walker hadn't been poking out. Her ball seemed to get stuck. It stopped, but Helen kept going, went right in that poor lady's lap. The wheelchair gave and she and Helen went down. Crushed her dead. She couldn't bear all the weight. Helen is fine. Her pride was hurt cause she fell, but that's all. I don't think she knows what she did. That lady was frail, like my Helen was at the end. They called her Miss Rose. I called my Helen, my sunflower. I got that bear to forget.

CHAPTER 6

PILOT PARTLY SUCKED OUT OF AIRLINER

A Passenger

It was quite a sight seeing them, two on one leg, one on another, their hair standing on end as if it wanted to follow, their clothes billowing like ghosts as they cheered each other on. With the noise, the wind, those masks, we knew right away what was at stake: A life, a plane full of lives. We sucked in the air of realization with enough force that you would have thought it might hold him in.

Need I say it: We were terrified. For me, there were no dear Gods, no life flashing. I had my compact out when it happened and I just sat there staring at myself, locked on my own image, on my own quivering face. I never knew I could hold such a look.

Now, when I'm in front of a mirror, I see that face I'd never seen before. When I walk out to face the day, it walks with me. It is as if I can't get off that plane, can't stop seeing.

The Co-Pilot

I knew what I had to do. I took control. I found an airport. I got her down. I didn't panic. When they ask their questions, I quietly answer knowing the world up there was a world gone mad—Tim hanging out, the yelling, the noise, the tangle of bodies next to me. It all strangely seemed far away as if in another place, beyond me, and I did and I did not hear it since I was the only sane one left.

But should I have done more? Windows are not on my check list! I had to take the controls, assume command, accept the responsibility. I knew what I had to do. I couldn't be reaching for Tim.

Another Passenger

I just can't believe it! I can't! A window coming out! Him stuck! Of all things! I can tell you, I'll never get back on one. Never! Not even if you paid me! Imagine! A window coming out!

A Flight Attendant

When they talk about our heroics, I listen. After all, I was one of the ones who kept him in. I came to his aid, I held on, my arms aching and my head pounding with the pressure. But only after the others called did I go to him and grab hold, not by choice but by their command. I knew there was a life to save. I hung on, not for him, but for me. My heroics were born of necessity.

The Pilot

I was suspended, half in and half out, the top half flapping like a flag, the bottom secured by the attendants' dedicated grasp. They hung on, pulled in the tug-of-war with the air. It must have been a sight. It sounded like champagne opening when the window popped off. It must have looked as if I was trying to dive into open space, to celebrate being free from earth, but my mind was on the flashing world below.

As my head bashed from side to side and my spine bent back from the force, I returned to my childhood home, hanging from the old tree in our yard, slipping, then calling to my mother to save me from branches too high. And at 24,000 feet I saw once again her open hands, reach up to deliver me, not with the crazed clasp of those clinging on below my waist, but with gentle caresses against my cheek until all was air, air.

CHAPTER 6

PIT BULLS

I just wanted a little breeze in the house
before my shows came on,
so I opened the front door.
In they came, straight at me,
as if they had been waiting
for weeks for this moment.
Their eyes were slits
from the night, their mouths
were nothing but teeth.
It didn't seem
real, even after, they pulled me
from my wheelchair
and bit into my dead legs.
Blood poured from where flesh once was.
It didn't seem real,
even after, as if words might matter,
I told them to shoo.
That's when one took to my foot.
It didn't
seem real, after I somehow
grabbed the phone and called 911
and heard the emergency operator say,

"Get rid of those dogs, ma'am,
I can't hear you."

SPILLS

Sure, I was tempted when it happened. They all came in, all ten of them, splashing around, kicking their legs. It was hard to resist, them not being the usual fare, but I had just eaten and the thought of all that leather and rubber stuck in my teeth, well, I just decided to pass. If barefooted, it might have been another matter.

Truth be told, it wasn't about food. When the catwalk collapsed in my tank, I had my chance. Everyone rushed to the glass. Everyone was there, watching, waiting to see what I'd do. But I settled under the coral that's too close to the side of the south wall. I keep telling myself that I was startled, simply played it safe, that I was smart. But if I had taken just one foot or an arm, gone for a soft side, maybe dragged a child to the bottom before spitting it out, then they'd know that their glass can cage, but it can't contain. When they'd see me circle, they wouldn't turn away, bored, but they'd linger, filling their heads with me.

CHAPTER 6

NO RHYME OR REASON

He stands on the porch smoking a cigarette
With each puff, he remembers what he can't forget

The moon smears itself into the clay
The train's distant moan fades away

The whale swims onto the empty beach
Feels useless hands, their desperate reach

The dead branch in the tree—brown against green
Kids in the parking lot—nothing but mean

The shoemaker's cash gets one last tally
The broken glass waits in the alley

The soldier's leg hung by a single thread
He spoke only once, wishing he were dead

The dull crack of morning light shines
Not a single star stays behind

He goes inside and shuts the door.

OLD BALD MEN

I join their ranks
belly leading
back aching
golf club swinging

I can't imagine how
we took charge.

CHAPTER 6

HOW THE WORLD BREAKS

When the world would break,
he would break out in tears.
Where his tears would fall
flowers would soon follow,
but the world would break again
and his tears would again fall.
He wanted to break this circle
of despair, hope, and again despair
so he broke himself. His eyes shut.
There were no more tears.
The world continued to break.

TELL ME THE TRUTH

1.

Partner 1: Tell me the truth.
Partner 2: I can't.
Partner 1: Why not?
Partner 2: It would do too much damage to us.
Partner 1: We're damaged now. Tell me what you're thinking.
Partner 2: I'm thinking you don't want to hear what I have to say.
Partner 1: Fuck you.
Partner 2: See what I mean.

2.

Partner 1: Tell me the truth.
Partner 2: I'm trying.
Partner 1: Well, try harder. You can't keep things from me.
Partner 2: I'm trying to be exact, to say what I want to say.
Partner 1: Just spit it out.
Partner 2: If I do that, I might regret saying what I've said.
Partner 1: So you're saying you're not telling me the whole truth.
Partner 2: I didn't say that.
Partner 1: That's what it sounds like to me.

3.

Partner 1: Tell me the truth.
Partner 2: You really want the truth.
Partner 1: Yes.
Partner 2: It will be the end of us.
Partner 1: Well, I can't live knowing you're hiding something from me.
Partner 2: We could just forget all this.
Partner 1: I won't live with something buried between us.
Partner 2: Okay. You asked for it.

CHAPTER 6

4.

Partner 1: Tell me the truth.
Partner 2: I'm not sure what the truth is.
Partner 1: I think you do. You just don't want to say it.
Partner 2: Whatever I say won't get it right.
Partner 1: You're playing games with me. Just tell me.
Partner 2: I'll tell you a version.
Partner 1: How many versions are there?
Partner 2: I'm not sure.
Partner 1: You asshole.

5.

Partner 1: Tell me the truth.
Partner 2: I'll tell you, but you have to promise you won't get upset.
Partner 1: I can't promise that.
Partner 2: Then I won't tell you.
Partner 1: I can't predict how I'm going to respond before I hear it.
Partner 2: I don't want you to go all ballistic on me.
Partner 1: You've made such a big deal out of this. Now you have to tell me.
Partner 2: No, not now. You have to forget it.
Partner 1: Forget it? After what you've said? You got to be kidding me.
Partner 2: I'm not saying a word.

6.

Partner 1: Tell me the truth.
Partner 2: No.
Partner 1: What do you mean "no"?
Partner 2: I mean no. Not a word.
Partner 1: You can't do that.
Partner 2: That's the decision I've made.
Partner 1: That's not fair.
Partner 2: Sorry.
Partner 1: Sorry isn't enough.

7.

Partner 1: Tell me the truth.
Partner 2: There's nothing to tell.
Partner 1: Then why are you being so secretive.
Partner 2: I'm not being secretive. There are no secrets.
Partner 1: What are you hiding?
Partner 2: I'm not hiding anything.
Partner 1: You're lying to me. I can tell when you're lying.
Partner 2: I'm not lying.
Partner 1: I don't believe you.
Partner 2: I swear.

8.

Partner 1: Tell me the truth.
Partner 2: Are you sure you want to hear it?
Partner 1: Why wouldn't I want to know?
Partner 2: Because it will hurt you.
Partner 1: Why do you say that?
Partner 2: Because I know you and this would upset you.
Partner 1: I can deal with it.
Partner 2: I don't think you can.
Partner 1: It's that bad.
Partner 2: Let's just say it isn't anything you want to hear.
Partner 1: Are you sure?
Partner 2: Yes, I'm sure.
Partner 1: Okay, forget it.
Partner 2: I think that's smart.
Partner 1: But now I'll always wonder.
Partner 2: That's better than knowing.

9.

Partner 1: Tell me the truth.
Partner 2: You tell me what you have to say first.
Partner 1: No. I don't want what I say to influence you.
Partner 2: It would help me know what you want me to focus on.

CHAPTER 6

Partner 1: I want you to focus on the truth. Start at the beginning. I've got all night.
Partner 2: You don't want to hear about all this garbage.
Partner 1: Yes, I do. Every detail.
Partner 2: This could take all night.
Partner 1: Go ahead. Begin.

10.

Partner 1: Tell me the truth.
Partner 2: I rather not.
Partner 1: Right now, I don't much care what you rather or rather not do.
Partner 2: I can do what I want.
Partner 1: Yes, you can, but I won't be here if you do what you want.
Partner 2: You're saying, I have no choice.
Partner 1: You got a choice, but you better pick the right one.
Partner 2: Are you threatening me?
Partner 1: Call it what you want, but you have to tell me everything.
Partner 2: I'd rather not.

11.

Partner 1: Tell me the truth.
Partner 2: I've told you the truth.
Partner 1: Stop lying to me.
Partner 2: I'm not lying.
Partner 1: Yes, you are.
Partner 2: No, really. I'm telling you the truth.
Partner 1: I don't believe you.
Partner 2: What can I say to make you believe me?
Partner 1: The truth.

12.

Partner 1: Tell me the truth.
Partner 2: The truth is best where it is—hidden, buried.
Partner 1: We have to dig it up.
Partner 2: Digging it up won't do any good.
Partner 1: I can't live in the dark any longer. It's eating at me.
Partner 2: It might devour you if we dig it up.
Partner 1: I'll take my chances.
Partner 2: Are you sure?
Partner 1: Yes. I want the truth. No more lies.

CHAPTER 6

CLUES TO THE POSSIBILITY OF HEARING THE TRUTH

1.

Body
with open arms
eyes ready to meet eyes
mouth no longer silent, saying
sorry.

2.

Body
nervous, in pain
perhaps a twitch, a tear
showing the toll of being caught
in lies.

3.

Body
released, empty
looking up, just waiting,
wanting an understanding nod,
your hand.

TEARS

Having arranged to meet Liz in the lobby of an old New York hotel before they would join their friends for a night of dancing, Rachel found herself standing in front of an old, dusty painting. She was not sure why she was drawn to it. Its primary colors were dull. Dominating the painting was an oblong shape that reminded her of a tear. It was red, moving from left center to the bottom right in soft curving lines. In the background were more curving shapes in various colors, but none were formed like a tear. She looked to see if the painting had been signed or named, but she saw no evidence of either.

"What are you looking at?" her friend Liz asks, coming up from behind.

"Oh, hi," Rachel says and gives Liz a quick hug. "Look at this picture."

Liz glances up and offers her critique. "It doesn't do much for me."

"Don't you see all that is in that tear moving across the canvas?" Rachel says in a quiet voice.

"All I see is a big red blob," Liz answers. "I did read the other day scientists found that tears from different emotions have different chemicals. Tears of joy are different from tears of pain, and so on."

Still staring at the painting, Rachel barely whispers, "This one is filled with sadness, pain, and sorrow, so I guess it would be hard for the scientists to nail down."

"Come on, let's get out of here. Everyone will be waiting," Liz urges.

"You go ahead. Maybe I'll join you later, but right now I'm just not up to it."

"Oh, come on. It will be fun. We'll laugh until we have tears in our eyes."

Rachel offers Liz a small smile and shakes her head no. "I just need to stay here a bit longer. I need to be with this painting."

"Okay, but promise you'll come join us. You know where we'll be," Liz says and after another quick hug, turns and leaves.

CHAPTER 6

Rachel continued looking at the painting. She was falling deeper and deeper into its world.

A bellhop had been watching Rachel since she came into the lobby. He slowly approaches her. "If you look at that for too long, you'll find yourself depressed. After working here for a few a months, I told myself I couldn't look at it anymore. It got to me too much."

Rachel hears him speak, but it's as if the voice is from inside her head. She almost feels a tear run down her face.

REPAIR

Between both sides
of the tear

some would say
truth tries

to reassemble itself.
The torn

finds its own form
by forgetting what once was.

It struggles
to slip by its past.

History is the weight it refuses
as it weaves its way,

it surprises itself
by the possible,

shapes itself into contentment
until, once again,

it becomes a tear.

CHAPTER 6

HE

Sitting next to the man
with the white beard,
I don't speak.
He seems pleasant
as he watches me write.
I'll make him into words
flowing from his wiry whiskers
floating on his sweet breath
matching his plaid coat.
I'll create his participle
dangling from his ear
hanging in good cheer.
I'll let his adverbs
dance quickly
his adjectives fall in
an array of seamless sentences.
I'll become his possessive.
We will verb together, without
speaking, without ever
knowing names.
I'll write his pronoun.

THE TRUTH

Collects and arranges itself one word at a time, selecting from all its possible choices.

Seeks an accepting ear.

Lives in opposition to the lie, constantly pushing exaggerations, excesses, and excuses away, exposing slights, schemes, and buried secrets, and fighting off fabrications, falsifications, and fakery.

Stands in the sunlight, bare, ready to hold its ground.

Wants itself.

Eats mouthful after mouthful, always wary of a disagreeable sauce.

Walks in everyday shoes, walks, most of the time, with ease; wears boots only when the shit gets deep.

Shields itself from slips of the tongue, slips into the dark, slips into sorrow.

Competes against the lie, and, sometimes, lets the lie win.

Plants itself in time, turning the possible into the real.

Discovers itself in the telling.

Rides on history's back.

Marches on, believing in itself, singing its own song, until it stumbles on its own convictions.

Watches how it's treated, prefers the company of those who believe, with some caution, it should be honored.

CHAPTER 6

Ducks when it may cause more harm than good, when hiding is a generous act, a kindness without negative consequences.

Falls apart when its nails come loose.

Forgets its case for being itself.

Loves its teller, places the teller under its care.

Rings true to itself when it's finished remembering.

Gathers all that it can contain.

Breathes through the mouth of the dragon, setting fire to the false.

Balances maybe against habit.

Reveals itself at its own pace.

Leads by example.

Jars the unexpecting, destabilizes until the surprising becomes settled.

Gloats when the majority champions its cause.

Pleases by its naming, by the order it keeps, by the rules it insists are followed.

Predicts the future, smug as the number one, believing that when tomorrow comes, everything will be the same.

Muscles beyond feeble attempts hoping for approval, weak cases trying to impress, and vacuous doctrine calling for followers.

Remembers when it was a lie.
Trades confidence for evidence.

Vanishes when power has other interests.

Entangles itself, like an overgrown garden, flowering in unanticipated places.

Is what I've tried to tell.

A FINAL TRUTH

I don't know what else to say. I think I've told you the truth the best I could. Whether I was sharing details from my personal life, trying to enter the psychological space of some person other than myself, or pulling from life experiences to create characters that rang true, I was never intentionally dishonest. I felt throughout that if we were to have a meaningful connection between the two of us, I owed you at least that much. I never wanted you to think I might be lying to you. That's not a good foundation for a relationship. You may not know, however, who was speaking when. That's why I've included "Appendix A: An Accounting by Genre of the Author's Truth Telling." I realize this may not matter to you, but it's there in case you're interested.

I have to admit I'm of two minds about including Appendix A. On the one hand, I wanted you to read each piece for the truth it may tell, regardless of the type of text it might be. On the other hand, I believe knowing the kind of communicative act you might be engaging influences how you process it, what sense you make of it. Genre and truth are hard to separate, and knowing what's what, provides some comfort. Nevertheless, I hope you found leaving the what's what question somewhat open across the various pieces in this book useful to you as you considered the role of truth telling in your reading and in your life. At a minimum, I would be disappointed if you didn't leave this book feeling that truth telling is rather slippery business, despite all the efforts we make to tell the truth. The truth of our social and communicative lives is deeply contingent. "Appendix B: Engagements" offers some questions in case you might want to think about the issue of truth telling a bit more.

In this final moment we have together, I would like to share one more thought from the stance of the writer. I want to call upon a familiar argument in writing circles, an argument you probably have already heard: The fiction and nonfiction writer's job is to tell the truth. It's an act of trying to get the words right, of trying to make tales ring true. It's the struggle, the needed perseverance, to discover what you, as a writer, need to say. It's finding those words that seem, at least for a moment in time, to settle into a satisfactory account. It's those times when a piece shapes, perhaps to your surprise, what you come to believe. It's the personal epiphany, the pleasure of thinking that a possible answer is at hand. That's the truth I want to share with you now.

APPENDIX A

AN ACCOUNTING BY GENRE OF THE AUTHOR'S TRUTH TELLING

CHAPTER 1: RELATIONAL LOGICS

Text   Genre   Comment

Text	Genre	Comment
Wanting	Flash Fiction	Fictional
Now	Poem	Based upon life experience
Performance	Poem	Based upon newspaper report
The Ideal Partner	Lyric Essay	Based upon life experience
Spitting Together	Monologue/Flash Fiction	Based upon newspaper report
Waiting	Poem	Fictional
First Love	Flash Fiction	Fictional
When I Came Home	Poem	Based upon life experience
Mutual Embraces	Lyric Essay	Based upon life experience
One Night Stand	Poem	Fictional
Cruelties	Micro-Dramas	Fictional
Lone Deer	Poem	Based upon newspaper report
Finis	Poem	Based upon life experience
Custody Battle	Monologues/Flash Fiction	Based upon newspaper report
Against	Poem	Based upon life experience
Asking	Poem	Fictional
Moving	Poem	Based upon life experience
Getting It Right	Flash Fiction	Fictional
Olga	Poem	Based upon life experience
Another Year	One Act Play	Fictional

APPENDIX A

CHAPTER 2: CHILDHOOD AND ADOLESCENT DANGERS

Text   Genre   Comment

Text	Genre	Comment
Starbucks	Poem	Based upon newspaper report
Suffocating	Poem	Based upon newspaper report
Book Case	One Act Play	Fictional
Curiosity	Literary Nonfiction	Based upon cultural clichés
Toddler Found in the Schoolyard	Poem	Based upon newspaper report
Boy	Monologues/Flash Fiction	Based upon newspaper report
Long Range	Poem	Based upon life experience
Childhood Distress	Stories/Personal Narratives	Based upon life experience
Don't	Literary Nonfiction	Based upon cultural clichés
Dead Man's Alley	Story/Personal Narrative	Based upon life experience
Bobby	Poem	Based upon life experience
Back Yard	Monologue/Personal Narrative	Based upon life experience

School Instruction
   Spanish Class
   The Triplets
   Chicken Shit
	
	Story/Personal Narrative
	Short Story/Flash Fiction
	Story/Personal Narrative
		
		Based upon life experience
		Fictional
		Based upon life experience

Manacle Mom	Poem	Based upon newspaper repot
Fifteen High School Micro-Dramas	Micro-Dramas	Mix of the fictional and non-fictional (autobiographical)
Stuck	Monologue/Flash Fiction	Based upon newspaper report
Drinking	Story/Personal Narrative	Based upon life experience
In Search of a Drinking Song	Poem	Fictional

CHAPTER 3: JESUS CHRONICLES

Text	Genre	Comment
For the Children	Flash Fiction	Fictional
Kudzu Communion	Monologue/Flash Fiction	Fictional
No More	Poem	Fictional
Church Going	Short Stories/ Narratives	Section 1 & 3: Fictional Section 2: Personal narrative based upon life experience
Christian Spinoffs	Literary Nonfiction	Based upon religious clichés
Body to Body	Poem	Fictional
Judgment	Monologue/Flash Fiction	Based upon newspaper report
Priest Confesses	Poem	Based upon newspaper report
Following God's Law	Monologue/Flash Fiction	Based upon newspaper report
A Christian Education	Short Story	Fictional
Prayers	Prayers	Fictional
The Trick	Monologue/Flash Nonfiction	Based upon life experience
You Can't Boo Jesus	One Act Play	Fictional

APPENDIX A

CHAPTER 4: CRIMINAL TALES

Text   Genre   Comment

Text	Genre	Comment
The Drugstore Heist	Short Story	Based upon life experience
Woman Charged	Poem	Based upon newspaper report
Man Ordered	Poem	Based upon newspaper report
The Interview	One Act Play	Fictional
The Criminal Mind	Literary Nonfiction	Based upon life experience
From the Bridge	Monologues/ Flash Fiction	Based upon newspaper report
Railway Shooting	Monologue/ Flash Fiction	Based upon newspaper report
Crimes of United States Politicians	Literary Nonfiction	Based upon news reports
Twin	Poem	Based upon newspaper report
Shotgun Murder	Monologue/Flash Fiction	Based upon newspaper report
Ruined Day	Poem	Based upon newspaper report
An Open Letter to the Person Who Broke into my House	Letter	Fictional
Painted Body Parts	Monologue/Flash Fiction	Based upon newspaper report
On the One Year Anniversary of Ferguson	Poem	Fictional Speaker/ nonfictional list
Staying Inside	Monologue/Flash Fiction	Fictional
Last Words	Monologue/Flash Fiction	Fictional
When Those We Call Great Fall	Poem	Based upon life experience and news reports

AN ACCOUNTING BY GENRE OF THE AUTHOR'S TRUTH TELLING

CHAPTER 5: AGING, ILLNESS, AND DEATH LESSONS

Text   Genre   Comment

Text	Genre	Comment
The Worry List	Prose Poem	Based upon life experience
Surfaces	Monologue/Flash Fiction	Based upon newspaper report
Woman Hospitalized	Poem	Based upon newspaper report
On Going Nuts	Monologue/Flash Fiction	Fictional
Going Home	Poem	Based upon life experience
When	Lyric Essay	Based upon life experience
The End of an Academic Career	Autoethnography	Based upon life experience
Old Bones	Monologue/Flash Fiction	Fictional
Still Waiting	Poem	Based upon life experience
How to Watch Your Mother Die	Poem	Based upon life experience
Cremation Endings	Monologues/Flash Fiction	Fictional
Morgue	Poem	Based upon newspaper report
Bien	Poem	Based upon newspaper report
Still There	Poem	Based upon life experience
Ritual	Poem	Based upon life experience
Passing	Poem	Based upon life experience
The Grave	Poem	Fictional
Always Becoming	Literary Nonfiction	Based upon life experience

APPENDIX A

CHAPTER 6: TELLING TRUTHS

Text					Genre			Comment

Text	Genre	Comment
American Beauty	Monologue/Flash Fiction	Based upon newspaper report
Ken Doll Turns Forty	Poem	Based upon newspaper report
Playing the Game	Monologue/Flash Fiction	Fictional
The Lies Couples Keep	Micro-Dramas	Fictional
Nailed Down	Monologue/Flash Fiction	Fictional
On the Streets	Poem	Based upon life experience
Neighbor	Poem	Based upon life experience
The Teacher	Monologue/Personal Narrative	Based upon life experience
Border Crossing	Poem	Based upon life experience
Helen	Monologue/Flash Fiction	Based upon newspaper report
Pilot Partly Sucked Out of Airliner	Monologues/Flash Fiction	Based upon newspaper report
Pit Bulls	Poem	Based upon newspaper report
Spills	Monologue/Flash Fiction	Based upon newspaper report
No Rhyme or Reason	Poem	Based upon life experience
Old Bald Men	Poem	Based upon life experience
How the World Breaks	Poem	Fictional
Tell Me the Truth	Micro-Dramas	Fictional
Clues to the Possibility of Hearing the Truth	Poem	Based upon life experience
Tears	Short Story	Fictional
Repair	Poem	Based upon life experience
He	Poem	Based upon life experience
The Truth	Lyric Essay	Based upon life experience

APPENDIX B

ENGAGEMENTS

Appendix B is designed to further your engagement with *If the Truth Be Told*. It invites you to consider questions related to the book in regard to its chapters' subjects, its dealings with issues of truth, and its consideration of fictional and nonfictional writing as well as writing as a research method. Some of the questions address a general audience and some target readers with more academic interests. The Appendix first offers questions that can be asked of all the chapters followed by questions related to specific chapters.

QUESTIONS ACROSS CHAPTERS

1. Select a chapter and consider what themes emerged from the included pieces. Do you feel these texts provide a full or complete account of the subject? If not, what seems to be missing? What additional ideas might be included to offer a more sufficient picture?
2. Putting together what is given in a chapter and what ideas you might have added, how might you argue that these themes do or do not stand as research? Argue for or against the idea that each selection is data related to the chapter's subject?
3. Does the use of literature add or take away your trust in what is presented? Does it matter if the piece is fictional or nonfictional? Explain your reasoning.
4. What are you willing to claim about truth telling? Can the truth be told? What makes you believe one account but not another? What selections ring true to your experience? What ones seem to lack credibility?

5. Why do people lie? Does anyone benefit from a lie? Are there examples in the book that support your perspective?
6. What does literature add to an understanding of human experience that a more traditional scholarly essay would be unlikely to include? What does a more traditional scholarly essay add to an understanding of human experience that literature might obscure?
7. If you were to add a piece from your own experience for each of the chapters, what would you write? What genre would you be most likely to select to tell each of your tales? Why those forms? Would you be more likely to turn to fictional or nonfictional accounts?
8. How are ethics and truth telling related? What ethical obligations do you feel to tell the truth when speaking to others? Are there some things that people should never share or only share with loved ones? Is it ethical when writing nonfiction to alter or omit "facts" in order to make a better story? Is it ethical to create speakers who are justifying their horrific action?
9. Many of the autobiographical entries across the chapters point to the author's identity. What impression have you formed of the author? How has the author's identity influenced the construction of each chapter? If you were to write on the topic of each chapter, how might the chapters be constructed differently?
10. To what extent is language capable of capturing the truth? What is the difference between being true and being truthful?

CHAPTER SPECIFIC QUESTIONS

Chapter 1: Relational Logics

1. What does this chapter suggest to you about your own relationships? What pieces reflect a relational logic that you could see yourself using? What logics do you use to determine if you are in a good or bad relationship?
2. Several of the pieces point to what the speakers want in a relationship and several report on failed relationships? How does the chapter play with the tension between ideal desires and everyday reality?

What logics do you use to determine when to stay in a relationship and when to leave?
3. Identify your best and worst relationship. What made your best the best and what made your worst the worst?
4. If you wanted to write about a previous or current relationship, would you be ethically obligated to check with your partner before making your writing public?

Chapter 2: Childhood and Adolescent Dangers

1. What stories do you carry from your own childhood and adolescence that placed you in danger? How do you feel about these stories—are they troubling to you? Amusing?
2. Does the chapter make a case that the greatest danger to children is adults? What obligations do you feel parents should have in regard to their children?
3. In general, the chapter moves from early childhood through adolescence. How do early life dangers change over time? Are there behaviors you engaged in that you wish you hadn't? Has age made you wiser?
4. How might you write about your most dangerous physical or psychological childhood or adolescent experience? What might be the therapeutic value in writing about life experiences that placed you in danger? What might be the dangers of doing such writing?

Chapter 3: Jesus Chronicles

1. What selections or moments in the chapter align most closely with your understanding of good Christian practice? What selections or moments seems the most far removed from Christian principles? Does the chapter capture an adequate range of Christian sensibilities?
2. Do any of the entries seem offensive to you? If so, explain what makes you uncomfortable? What do you see as the risks of writing about your own faith?

APPENDIX B

3. How might someone who isn't of the Christian faith meet this chapter? Does the chapter present a picture of a person of faith that rings true regardless of what faith one might have?
4. How might you link your religious experience to the two previous chapters? In other words, how is your faith related to how you make sense of your relational life? What childhood or adolescent religious experiences felt dangerous to you?

Chapter 4: Criminal Tales

1. What behaviors described in the chapter seemed to you the most and least criminal?
2. What makes a behavior criminal? What laws do you feel you could break without feeling as if you had done anything wrong? What behaviors would you consider criminal even though they might be legal? Are tales about one's own criminal behaviors often self-serving?
3. Read "The Criminal Mind" again asking yourself what criminal acts have crossed your mind. What criminal thoughts would you be most reluctant to admit? If you wanted to write about your criminal behavior, what would you select? What would you avoid telling?
4. Identify a time when have you felt victimized. How would you describe your emotional responses? Did you find yourself wanting retribution? Did you find yourself working toward forgiveness?

Chapter 5: Aging, Illness, and Death Lessons

1. What lessons does the chapter offer in regard to dealing with aging, illnesses, and death? Do you find these lessons useful as you consider your own life?
2. How might you describe your relationship to your own body, its aging, its illnesses, its inevitable death? Are there things that you could once do with ease that you no longer can? Have you had to face serious illnesses, had close calls with your own death? What gives you the most worries?
3. The piece, "The End of an Academic Career," I classified in Appendix A as autoethnography, a research method used by scholars that calls

upon the evocative to help make its case. Running the length of a typical essay in a scholarly journal, it serves as an example of an academic form that weds traditional research and literature. How does this piece function differently from other pieces within this book? What does it share in common with other entries?
4. In what ways does U.S. culture limit how you might write about death? What aspects of death does U.S. culture try to hide? What scripts are available to speak about death? What rituals are permitted, encouraged, and mandated? How does the economics of death influence how one might mourn?

Chapter 6: Truth Telling

1. This chapter is a mix of pieces about truth, some that address truth telling directly and some that represent speakers who come to some realization they see as truthful. Following the examples of those speakers who came to some realization, describe experiences in your life when some insight came to you as a truthful realization that you didn't have until that moment. How are those experiences similar to or different from the direct statements about truth telling in the chapter?
2. Remember a time when you felt someone was not telling you the truth? What happened in that person's telling that made you doubt him or her? What behaviors accompany truthful accounts?
3. What personal skills are needed to write the truth of someone else's experience?
4. The final sentence of Part 2 in the beginning introductory remarks ended with the comment that "the truth is elusive, contingent, difficult to nail down, but when spoken, always does or does not carry a personal sense of veracity." To what extent does this book convince you of that claim? How would you rewrite it to make it seem more truthful?

SUGGESTED READING

Adams, T. E. (2011). *Narrating the closet: An autoethnography of same-sex attraction.* Walnut Creek, CA: Left Coast Press.
Adams, T. E., Holman Jones, S., & Ellis, C. (Eds.). (2015). *Autoethnography: Understanding qualitative research.* Oxford: Oxford University Press.
Bochner, A. P. (2014). *Coming to narrative: A personal history of paradigm change in the human sciences.* Walnut Creek, CA: Left Coast Press.
Bochner, A. P., & Ellis, C. (Eds.). (2002). *Ethnographically speaking: Autoethnography, literature, and aesthetics.* Walnut Creek, CA: AltaMira Press.
Boylorn, R. M. (2013). *Sweetwater: Black women and narratives of resilience.* New York, NY: Peter Lang.
Busch, F. (Ed.). (1999). *Letters to a fiction writer.* New York, NY: W. W. Norton.
Cheney, T. A. R. (2001). *Writing creative nonfiction: Fiction techniques for crafting great nonfiction.* Berkeley, CA: Ten Speed Press.
Davie, C. S. (2014). *Conversations about qualitative communication research: Behind the scenes with leading scholars.* Walnut Creek, CA: Left Coast Press.
Defenbaugh, N. L. (2011). *Dirty tale: A narrative journey of the IBD body.* Cresskill, NJ: Hampton Press.
Denzin, N. K. (1997). *Interpretive ethnography: Ethnographic practices for the 21st century.* Thousand Oaks, CA: Sage.
Denzin, N. K., & Lincoln, Y. S. (Eds.). (2011). *The Sage handbook of qualitative inquiry.* Thousand Oaks, CA: Sage.
Dillard, A. (1982). *Living by fiction.* New York, NY: Harper & Row.
Ellis, C. (1995). *Final negotiations: A story of love, loss, and chronic illness.* Philadelphia, PA: Temple University Press.
Ellis, C. (2005). *The ethnographic I: A methodological novel about autoethnography.* Walnut Creek, CA: AltaMira Press.
Ellis, C. (2009). *Revision: Autoethnographic reflections on life and work.* Walnut Creek, CA: Left Coast Press.
Faulkner, S. L. (2009). *Poetry as method: Reporting research through verse.* Walnut Creek, CA: Left Coast Press.
Faulkner, S. L. (2013). *Inside relationships. A creative casebook in relational communication.* Walnut Creek, CA: Left Coast Press.
Faulkner, S. L. (2014). *Family stories, poetry, and women's work: Kit four, frog one (poems).* Rotterdam, The Netherlands: Sense Publishers.
Gale, K., & Wyatt, J. (2010). *Between the two: A nomadic inquiry into collaborative writing.* Newcastle upon Tyne: Cambridge Scholars Publishing.
Gingrich-Philbrook, C. (1998). What I 'know' about the story (for those about to tell personal narratives on stage). In S. J. Dailey (Ed.), *The future of performance studies: Visions and revisions* (pp. 298–300). Annandale, VA: National Communication Association.
Gingrich-Philbrook, C. (2001). Bite your tongue: Four songs of body and language. In L. C. Miller & R. J. Pelias (Eds.), *The green window: Proceeding of the Giant City conference on performative writing* (pp. 1–7). Carbondale, IL: Southern Illinois University.
Goldberg, N. (2000). *Thunder and lightning: Cracking open the writer's craft.* New York, NY: Bantam.

Goldberg, N. (2007). *Old friend far away: The practice of writing memoir*. New York, NY: Free Press.
Goldstein, T. (2013). *Zero tolerance and other plays: Disrupting xenophobia, racism and homophobia in school*. Rotterdam, The Netherlands: Sense Publishers.
Goodall, Jr., H. L. (1989). *Casing a promised land: The autobiography of an organizational detective as cultural ethnographer*. Carbondale, IL: Southern Illinois University Press.
Goodall, Jr., H. L. (1991). *Living in the rock n roll mystery: Reading context, self, and others as clues*. Carbondale, IL: Southern Illinois University Press.
Goodall, Jr., H. L. (1996). *Divine signs: Connecting spirit to community*. Carbondale, IL: Southern Illinois University Press.
Goodall, Jr., H. L. (2000). *Writing the new ethnography*. Walnut Creek, CA: AltaMira.
Goodall, Jr., H. L. (2008). *Writing qualitative inquiry: Self, story, and academic life*. Walnut Creek, CA: Left Coast Press.
Goodall, Jr., H. L. (2010). *Counter narrative: How progressive academics can challenge extremists and promote social justice*. Walnut Creek, CA: Left Coast Press.
Gutkind, L. (2012). *You can't make this stuff up: The complete guide to writing creative nonfiction—From memoir to literary journalism and everything in between*. Boston, MA: Da Capo/Lifelong Books.
Halley, J. O. (2012). *The parallel lives of women and cows*. New York, NY: Palgrave MacMillan.
Harris, A. (2014). *Critical plays: Embodied research for social change*. Rotterdam, The Netherlands: Sense Publishers.
Hemley, R. (1994). *Turning life into fiction*. Cincinnati, OH: Story Press.
Holman Jones, S. (2007). *Torch singing: Performing resistance and desire from Billie Holiday to Edith Piaf*. Landam, MD: AltaMira Press.
Holman Jones, S., Adams, T. E., & Ellis C. (Eds.). (2013). *Handbook of autoethnography*. Walnut Creek, CA: Left Coast Press.
hooks, b. (1997). *Wounds of passion: A writing life*. New York, NY: Henry Holt.
hooks, b. (1999). *Remembered rapture: The writer at work*. New York, NY: Henry Holt.
Karr, M. (2015). *The art of memoir*. New York, NY: HarperCollins.
Kitchen, J. (Ed.). (2005). *Short takes: Brief encounters with contemporary nonfiction*. New York, NY: W. W. Norton.
Knowles, J. G., & Coles, A. L. (Eds.). (2008). *Handbook of the arts in qualitative inquiry: Perspectives, methodologies, examples, and issues*. Los Angeles, CA: Sage.
Kraft, R. N. (2014). *Violent accounts: Understanding the psychology of perpetrators through South Africa's truth and reconciliation commission*. New York, NY: New York University Press.
Kuntz, A. M. (2015). *The responsible methodologist: Inquiry, truth-telling, and social justice*. Walnut Creek, CA: Left Coast Press.
Lamott, A. (1994). *Bird by bird: Some instruction on writing and life*. New York, NY: Anchor.
Leavy, P. (2013a). *Fiction as research practice: Short stories, novellas, and novels*. Walnut Creek, CA: Left Coast Press.
Leavy, P. (2013b). *American circumstance*. Rotterdam, The Netherlands: Sense Publishers.
Leavy, P. (2015). *Low-fat love* (expanded anniversary edition). Rotterdam, The Netherlands: Sense Publishers.
Lockford, L. (2004). *Performing femininity: Rewriting gender identity*. Landam, MD: AltaMira Press.

Miller, B., & Paola, S. (2012). *Tell it slant: Creating, refining, and publishing creative nonfiction.* New York, NY: McGraw Hill.
Minge, J. M., & Zimmerman, A. L. (2013). *Concrete and dust: Mapping the sexual terrains of Los Angeles.* New York, NY: Routledge.
Moss, S. (Ed.). (1995). *The world's shortest stories.* San Luis Obispo, CA: New Times Press.
Munoz, K. L. (2014). *Transcribing silence: Culture, relationships, and communication.* Walnut Creek, CA: Left Coast Press.
Pelias, R. J. (1999). *Writing performance: Poeticizing the researcher's body.* Carbondale, IL: Southern Illinois University Press.
Pelias, R. J. (2004). *A methodology of the heart: Evoking academic & daily life.* Walnut Creek, CA: AltaMira.
Pelias, R. J. (2011). *Leaning: A poetics of personal relations.* Walnut Creek, CA: Left Coast Press.
Pelias, R. J. (2014). *Performance: An alphabet of performative writing.* Walnut Creek, CA: Left Coast Press.
Pineau, E. L. (2000). *Nursing mother* and articulating absence. *Text and Performance Quarterly, 20,* 1–19.
Pineau, E. L. (2011). Intimacy, empathy, activism: A performative engagement with children's wartime art. In N. K. Denzin & M. D. Giardina (Eds.), *Qualitaitve inquiry and global crises* (pp. 199–217). Walnut Creek, CA: Left Coast Press.
Poulos, C. N. (2009). *Accidental ethnography: An inquiry into family secrecy.* Walnut Creek, CA: Left Coast Press.
Richardson, L. (1997). *Fields of play: Constructing an academic life.* New Brunswick, NJ: Rutgers University Press.
Richardson, L. (2013). *After a fall: A sociomedical sojourn.* Walnut Creek, CA: Left Coast Press.
Shapard, R., & Thomas, J. (Eds.). (1986). *Sudden fiction: American short-short stories.* Layton, UT: Peregrine Smith Book.
Smartt Gullion, J. (2014). *October birds: A novel about pandemic influenza, infection control, and first responders.* Rotterdam, The Netherlands: Sense Publishers.
Speedy, J. (2015). *Staring at the park: A poetic autoethnographic inquiry.* Walnut Creek, CA: Left Coast Press.
Spry, T. (2011). *Body, paper, stage: Writing and performing autoethnography.* Walnut Creek, CA: Left Coast Press.
Stafford, K. (2003). *The muses among us.* Athens, GA: University of Georgia Press.
Tamas, S. (2013). *Life after leaving: The remains of spousal abuse.* Walnut Creek, CA: Left Coast Press.
Tillmann-Healy, L. M. (2001). *Between gay and straight: Understanding friendship across sexual orientation.* Walnut Creek, CA: AltaMira.
Tillmann, L. M. (2015). *In solidarity: Friendship, family, and activism beyond gay and straight.* New York, NY: Routledge.
Weems, M. E. (2015). *Blackeyed: Plays and monologues.* Rotterdam, The Netherlands: Sense Publishers.
Wyatt, J., & Adams, T. (Eds.). (2014). *On (writing) families: Autoethnographies of presence and absence, love and loss.* Rotterdam, The Netherlands: Sense Publishers.
Zingaro, L. (2009). *Speaking out: Storytelling for social change.* Walnut Creek, CA: Left Coast Press.

ABOUT THE AUTHOR

Ronald J. Pelias taught performance studies from 1981–2013 in the Department of Communication Studies at Southern Illinois University, Carbondale, IL. He is currently teaching as an adjunct professor at the University of Louisiana, Lafayette, LA. He works on the stage primarily as a director and on the page as a writer committed to non-traditional forms of scholarly representation. His most recent books exploring qualitative methods are *Leaning: A Poetics of Personal Relations* (2011) and *Performance: An Alphabet of Performative Writing* (2014).

Lightning Source UK Ltd.
Milton Keynes UK
UKOW06f1831310516

275324UK00001B/85/P